YORK N[

General Editors: Pr
of Stirling) & Profe
University of Beirut)

Rudyard Kipling

KIM

Notes by Valerie Gillies

MA M LITT (EDINBURGH)

 LONGMAN
YORK PRESS

YORK PRESS
Immeuble Esseily, Place Riad Solh, Beirut.

LONGMAN GROUP LIMITED
Burnt Mill,
Harlow, Essex

First published 1981
ISBN 0 582 78117 5
Printed in Hong Kong by
Wilture Enterprises (International) Ltd.

Contents

Part 1

Introduction

Life of Rudyard Kipling

RUDYARD KIPLING was born into a family in which the ideal of artistic craftsmanship was given great respect. His mother, Alice Macdonald, was a lively, witty woman who married a painter and sculptor, Lockwood Kipling, a knowledgeable and sensitive man. They had met on a picnic at Lake Rudyard in Staffordshire, which is the origin of the unusual name that they chose for their first child. Kipling was to describe them, towards the end of his life, as 'my Father with his sage Yorkshire outlook and wisdom; my Mother, all Celt and three-parts fire. . . .' These elements can be seen to unite in his own character.

His parents left for India immediately after their marriage, since his father was appointed to teach in the school of art in Bombay. Talented and ambitious, the Kiplings saw this minor appointment as their opportunity to make a place for themselves in Anglo-Indian society. ('Anglo-Indian' was the term which the British used to describe themselves in India.)

Born in Bombay in 1865, Rudyard Kipling was the apple of his parents' eyes, and enjoyed all the delights and privileges of an Anglo-Indian childhood. He spoke of his earliest memory being the colourful fruits of the bazaar seen on walks with his *ayah* and his bearer. Servants attended on his every wish, and he had an indulgent up-bringing. Indian nursery rhymes and songs were sung to him in the evenings, before he was taken indoors to see his parents and cautioned 'to speak English to Papa and Mama in the drawing-room', not the language in which he spoke and dreamt throughout the day. He described his English as a language roughly translated from the vernacular in which he thought. This intimate knowledge of India gained in childhood, this sense of the colour and lavish warmth of his first home, remained with him throughout his life, and it is his childhood love of India that he gives us in *Kim* especially.

One threat clouded the existence of every English family living in India, and that was the inevitable separation of children from their parents. It was thought that year after year of Indian heat would be bad for the health of English children and also that they could not in India acquire a knowledge of their own country and culture. Most of them were sent home to England to be educated. Kipling had to endure the circumstances of a childhood spent in exile from the family.

In his case, he was sent to live, not with relatives, but with a family who boarded the children of people living in India, for money. At six years of age, in a strange, cold country, his parents parted from him in the dawn, without an explanation about why he was being left, or for how long, but with the injunction that he was to learn to read and write soon, and send them letters. He had a sister who was left there too, but she seems not to have incurred the wrath of the lady of the house as much as Rudyard did. From being the wonder of his parents' world, the little sahib who ruled his own servants in an Anglo-Indian nursery, he became the black sheep of another household. He was precocious and full of life, but this was not appreciated by the woman in charge of him, for she made the next few years of his life a misery. She must have disliked him. Years went by in which his parents could not afford to return to England to see how their children were getting on.

Kipling learned to read, and read greedily, to escape the reality of the House of Desolation, as he called it. His strict foster-mother threatened him with hell-fire and eternal punishments for any wrong-doing. He said he was 'regularly beaten'. His poor eyesight grew worse, strained by the amount of reading that he did, until he was rapidly becoming half-blind. His little sister did what she could to protect him, but nothing could save such a sensitive child from thinking of this period of his life as a miserable imprisonment, with a child's acute sense of injustice. No wonder he would paint us the glorious picture of Kim's free wanderings, in his later life.

Each winter the children enjoyed a visit to their Aunt Georgie's home. This aunt, and another, were both married to artists. Kipling's happy visits were filled with affection, and also gave him a sense of the family preoccupation with art and good workmanship.

In the end, Kipling's failing eyesight was noticed by Aunt Georgie, who sent such an alarming letter to India that his mother sailed for home on the next ship. He was taken away from the House of Desolation to enjoy a carefree time with his mother, when he put behind him the hatred and despair he had experienced.

By now, Kipling was twelve years old and it was time for him to be sent to public school. Westward Ho!, his parents' choice, was selected, mainly because their close friend, Cormell Price, was headmaster there. His school prepared boys for the new, competitive Army Entrance Examination. Many of the boys had been born in India, many were soldiers' sons. The school was a simple, bleak place, the best advantage of which was its situation on the shore of the Atlantic. Discipline was harsh, but Kipling enjoyed the companionship of the other boys, as we know from the reminiscences of his schooldays which he worked up, later, into *Stalky & Co* (1899).

Kipling had special coaching from the headmaster in précis writing, which was to prove useful in journalism. Cormell Price had realised that he would become a literary man, and would not be sitting the Army examination. Price gave him the run of his own library, and Kipling was totally absorbed in reading, writing and editing. In this way a professional attitude towards writing was fostered in him at an early age. Meanwhile, Lockwood Kipling was planning to bring Rudyard out to India and find him employment on a newspaper, which he considered 'a man's life and a man's work'.

In the autumn of 1882 Rudyard Kipling left for India. He was almost seventeen, and he was in two minds about the move, for he wanted to be a literary man, and it seemed that he would only further that career by being in London, which was the centre of the literary world. He felt homesick for England by the time he passed Suez; he was not sure that he wanted to go on:

> Port Said marks a certain dreadful and exact division between East and West. Up to that point – it is a fringe of palms against the sky – the impetus of home memories and the echo of home interests carry the young man along very comfortably on his first journey. But at Suez one must face things . . . the world seems cruelly large and self-absorbed . . . . Then one begins to wonder when one will see those palms from the other side. Then the black hour of home-sickness . . . and weak despair shuts down with the smell of strange earth and the cadence of strange tongues.*

Yet, to his surprise, he felt an instant recognition when he reached Bombay:

> I found myself at Bombay where I was born, moving among sights and smells that made me deliver in the vernacular sentences whose meaning I knew not. Other Indian-born boys have told me how the same thing happened to them.
>
> There were yet three or four days' rail to Lahore, where my people lived. After these, my English years fell away, nor ever, I think, came back in full strength.

It was in Lahore that Kipling began his seven years' hard labour as a journalist, representing as he did one half of the editorial staff of the one daily paper of the Punjab, *The Civil and Military Gazette*. This

---

*All the quotations in this section are from Rudyard Kipling's autobiography, *Something of Myself*, Macmillan, London, 1937.

was heavy work, since he was busy between ten and fifteen hours every day:

> I had fever too, regular and persistent, to which I added for a while chronic dysentery. Yet I discovered that a man can work with a temperature of 104, even though next day he has to ask the office who wrote the article.

Kipling's strength lay in his discovery that he loved the shelter of family life. Now that the father, mother, brother and sister were together after so many years of separation, they called themselves 'The Family Square'. He began to write stories and poems, in the little spare time he had.

As a journalist, it was Kipling's job to know about everyone in India. He knew the members of the Punjab Club ('where I met none but picked men at their definite work – Civilians, Army, Education, Canals, Forestry, Engineering, Irrigation, Railways, Doctors and Lawyers') with their technical knowledge. He knew the people of the old city of Lahore and beyond, in 'liquor shops, gambling and opium dens . . . wayside entertainments . . . native dances'. He knew, too, the harsh life of the British soldier in India, and the hard-working but privileged life of the men who were the Government in India, the Viceroy and his English officials. Kipling travelled far afield for his newspaper, and in that way he got to know different regions of that 'great and beautiful land', where every fifty miles brings new differences of culture and landscape. He knew a real Mahbub Ali who visited him whenever he came to Lahore, with news of Asia beyond the Khyber Pass. His newspaper editor described this Pathan friend of Kipling's as 'indescribably filthy but with magnificent mien and features'.

The places Kipling knew best in India were the Muslim city of Lahore, and the British Government seat in Simla. He also visited the north-west frontier, going a little way into the Khyber Pass to be 'pot-shot' at. On one occasion, which he made use of later in *Kim*, he took a journey, for the sake of his health, along the Himalaya-Tibet road. Going into the great Hills was, to him,

> a revelation of 'all might, majesty, dominion, and power, henceforth and for ever', in colour, form and substance indescribable. A little of what I realised then came back to me in *Kim* . . . . On our last day, a thunderstorm, which had been at work a few thousand feet below us, rose to the level of the ridge we were crossing and exploded in our midst. We were all flung on our faces . . . .

Such were his first-hand experiences of that vast land. His experiences of the people of India were equally impressive:

Often the night got into my head . . . and I would wander till
dawn in all manner of odd places . . . in and about the narrow
gullies under the Mosque of Wazir Khan for the sheer sake of
looking. . . . One would come home, just as the light broke, in some
night-hawk of a hired carriage which stank of hookah-fumes,
jasmine-flowers, and sandalwood; and if the driver were moved to
talk, he told one a good deal. Much of real Indian life goes on in
the hot weather nights . . . .

These night-wanderings, and the insomnia which he rather enjoyed for
the visions and dreams it brought with it, stood him in good stead when
his newspaper needed extra copy. Kipling was the man to write space-
filling articles and stories, with his knowledge of the histories of Hindu,
Muslim, Sikh, Christian, Jew and Buddhist peoples. In 1885 he began
a series of tales in the *Civil and Military Gazette*, called *Plain Tales
from the Hills*. It was his practice, throughout his life, to be working
on some verse and some prose at the same time, and within a year
he published a collection of newspaper verses on Anglo-Indian life,
called *Departmental Ditties*. These were his first substantial books, and
they indicated that here was the first writer who could treat the life
of the Anglo-Indians as well as all the other races of India.

He moved to Allahabad, to work on *The Pioneer* newspaper, where
he wrote 'three-or-five thousand-word cartoons once a week'. His
'seven years' hard' labour as a journalist was nearly at an end, for he
was ready now to try his fortune as a professional writer in London.
Once his fame was established, he was to make one brief visit to
India, but he was never again to live in the land which taught him his
craft. This may have been because he 'felt each succeeding hot weather
more and more, and cowered in my soul as it returned'. His years in
India gave him rich material for his future work, and the knowledge
that they were the pivot of his experience is essential to an understanding of *Kim*.

He returned to London at the age of twenty-four, with ballads and
stories to sell. His fame had travelled before him, and he found himself a literary success overnight. His readers clamoured for more of
his work. Kipling's answer was that there was plenty more, and he
wrote busily. He also tried to come to terms with his own genius
by attempting full-length fiction in the form of the novel. He wrote
The Light that Failed (1891) – an apt title for his failed novel – and then
collaborated with Wolcott Balestier, a young American, in writing
The Naulakha (1892). While Kipling was on a round-the-world
voyage, he heard that his collaborator was dying. He returned to
Europe and married his dead friend's sister, Carrie, a strong-minded
and resilient woman.

The young Mr and Mrs Kipling went to America and settled for several years near her family in Vermont. It was there that he began writing his children's tales, when he was about thirty, and there he first had the idea of writing about the boy Kim. He laid *Kim* aside for other stories, and it was not until he was living in England again that *Kim* took shape fully, under the watchful eye of his father, who had retired after thirty years' work in India.

Throughout the middle years of his life, Kipling was involved in a copyright struggle with American publishers who were 'pirating' his authorised editions (that is, printing them without his authorisation). He had a feud, too, with his brother-in-law Beatty. These quarrels spoiled the idea of living in America for him. Finally, after his beloved six-year-old daughter had died in New York after the Kiplings had had a bad midwinter crossing of the Atlantic (Kipling too had pneumonia, but then recovered), he never returned to America.

Rudyard, Carrie and their two surviving children, Elsie and John, found their 'Very Own House', Bateman's, in Sussex. Here Kipling lived the life of a country gentleman, interesting himself in the improvement of his house and land, although he was also writing every day. He wrote a letter to C. E. Norton in 1902, saying:

Then we discovered England which we had never done before . . . and went to live in it. England is a wonderful land. It is the most wonderful of all foreign countries that I have ever been in. It is made up of trees and green fields and mud and the gentry . . . .

The Kiplings explored the English countryside in one of the earliest motor-cars. Kipling was always enthusiastic about new inventions, and wrote about machines of all kinds, railway engines, ships, aeroplanes and cars. He lived at Bateman's for the rest of his life, although the family spent many winters in the South African sunshine, where Cecil Rhodes had given Kipling a house for his use. Kipling was a war-reporter there during the Boer War, and he also travelled to Canada, Egypt, Sweden, Brazil and the West Indies in the latter part of his life. He was one of the best-travelled writers in that pre-jet age.

His response to the world that he saw overseas was a firm belief in England's duty to her Empire, and a knowledge that England's strength lay in her dominions abroad. He was the most vocal of patriots, and this made him unpopular with opponents of imperialism. Yet Kipling in his art, if not in his politics, could always see both sides of any question. He said in his poem 'The Two-Sided Man' that he owed this artistic vision 'to Allah Who gave me two/Separate sides to my head'.

Throughout his life he always wrote copiously, as a glance at the list of his complete works will show. Moreover, his art was constantly developing and maturing. *Kim,* published in 1901, was his most successful attempt at a novel. After it, he continued to perfect the short story form. The complex stories he wrote in his last years, such as 'Dayspring Mishandled', published in *Limits and Renewals* (1932), seem to many present-day critics to be the best things he ever wrote.

His only son, John, died in the First World War. The loss of little Josephine, and then of John, were the two great sorrows of his life. Kipling always adored children, and his *Just So Stories* (1902) had been told aloud to his own and their friends.

Written shortly before his death in 1936, his autobiographical sketch, *Something of Myself,* deals with his life from the point of view of his work. Always a reserved man, he gives us an edited version of his private life. A writer of genius, he makes this appeal to the readers who will come after him:

> If I have given you delight
>   By aught that I have done,
> Let me lie quiet in that night
>   Which shall be yours anon:
>
> And for the little, little span
>   The dead are borne in mind,
> Seek not to question other than
>   The books I leave behind.

When Kipling and his friend King George V died within a few days of each other, the deaths of these two wise old men seemed like the end of an era. And so it was.

Kipling had enjoyed a heyday of literary popularity among the late Victorians, and his works continued to be best-sellers for years and years. His first success in London, in 1890, came at a time when England had had peace at home for over thirty years. It was the high tide of Victorian achievement and yet none of the great Victorian writers remained to celebrate it. The writers of Queen Victoria's mature years had either finished their work or died. A great age of literary output was ceasing, and English literature was at a momentary pause. Kipling was the man of the moment, who took these years by storm, because he found his subject matter among his contemporaries in the working world around him. Fame and fortune were his for the rest of his life.

In every country his work was widely read during his life and for a quarter of a century after his death. His poetry was admired by all kinds of men and women, and he was the one author whose writing obviously suited the taste of his generation.

He always made it plain that he believed England's rule to be the best of all possible worlds for her overseas dominions. This caused the reading public to love him more than his political or literary critics.

In his youth he had been influenced by reading and re-reading the Bible. He was attracted to the writings of Daniel Defoe (1660–1731), John Bunyan (1628–88), Henry Fielding (1707–54), Charles Dickens (1812–70), William Makepeace Thackeray (1811–63) and Robert Louis Stevenson (1850–94). In poetry, he enjoyed Ralph Waldo Emerson (1803–82) and Walt Whitman (1819–92), the Americans. His thoughts were directed by Thomas Carlyle (1795–1881), John Ruskin (1819–1900) and Robert Browning (1812–89) in particular, in his schoolboy days. He read very widely for one who was always busy with his own writing and editing.

The poetry and prose which he wrote in his lifetime adds up to five romances, two hundred and fifty short stories, one thousand pages of verse, and plenty of other miscellaneous writings. He was devoted to work. His craftsmanship stands, for Kipling's art suffers from no time-lag when his works are read today.

A note on the text

The text of *Kim* was first published by Macmillan, London, in 1901. Today's Pan Classic edition was published by Pan Books, London, in association with Macmillan, London, 1976.

Part 2

Summaries
of KIM

A general summary

Kim is the story of a boy in India in the last decade of the nineteenth century. Born of Irish parents, Kim is an orphan when we meet him first, a waif of the streets who is familiar with every quarter of Lahore. The woman who kept the house where his father had died taking opium looks after him and dresses him in European clothes, but Kim changes out of these into Hindu or Mohammedan ones when it suits him. At the age of about thirteen he is already adept at these changes and disguises. On the day that his tale begins he is playing with other boys outside the museum in Lahore, when the unusual figure of a Tibetan lama approaches. None of the boys has ever seen anyone like him, and the reaction of the native sons of traditional Hindu and Mohammedan families is to be wary of the foreigner; but Kim is delighted to meet someone new, and wants to learn all about him. Kim has no prejudices, and leads the old man into the museum to meet the curator. The Tibetan and the Englishman are both scholars, and the lama tells him of his Search to find the River where the Lord Buddha's arrow fell.

Kim, listening to the story of the Search outside the door, decides to accompany the lama as his disciple. That night he leads the lama to the Kashmir Serai, where he has a friend, the horse-dealer Mahbub Ali. He hopes Mahbub will give him money for their journey, but Mahbub gives more than that – he gives an entrance to the Great Game of government agents. He tests Kim by sending him off with a very important piece of information. So it is that on the same day Kim begins the pilgrimage of the Search with the lama, he also begins to play the Game, by carrying his secret message concerning the 'pedigree of the white stallion'.

Besides, Kim has a Search of his own, for a Red Bull, according to his father. Accompanying the lama on the train to Umballa, he takes care of him as a *chela*, or disciple, should, begging for their food and for ticket money from their kindly fellow-passengers. But as soon as the lama is safe in a hospitable household, Kim hurries off to deliver his message. He waits to see its effect, and hears the Commander-in-Chief order out eight thousand troops as a result. Back with the lama that same evening, a Brahmin priest casts Kim's horoscope and sees in it the sign of War, as well as the Bull. Kim, who has previously been called the Little Friend of all the World, is now also the Friend of the Stars.

He and the lama travel on, across the farmlands, looking for the River. They are befriended by an old rissaldar, a soldier from the times of the Mutiny. He guides them on to the Grand Trunk Road, which they will follow because it passes over many streams; any of these streams might be the one for which the lama is looking. They join the retinue of a sahiba, the old widow of a small hill rajah. She wishes the lama to be her priest and travel with her to her house near Saharunpore. Journeying with her procession, Kim and his lama turn aside to sit in a mango grove near sunset, when suddenly a whole regiment appears and makes camp. Their flag is a Red Bull, the sign of Kim's father's regiment, the Mavericks. Kim watches them in the dark, but is captured. Kim always wore his father's certificates in an amulet round his neck. These are discovered, and Father Victor, the Mavericks' priest, remembers Kimball O'Hara and realises that this must be his son. The lama, understanding that Kim is really a sahib and must go back to his own people, promises to remain with the Kulu woman, the sahiba from Saharunpore, until Kim's fate is settled.

Kim is not allowed to escape and resents being kept prisoner in the barracks at Umballa while the regiment is ordered to war, as he had 'prophesied' for them. He sends a letter to Mahbub Ali, asking him for help, and sure enough the big Pathan meets him on Umballa race-course, and introduces him to Colonel Creighton, a man whom Kim recognises as the sahib to whom he brought the 'war-making letter'. Meanwhile the lama has sent Father Victor a letter promising to pay three hundred rupees a year for Kim's schooling at St Xavier's. Colonel Creighton arranges to take Kim there, but on the way to Lucknow, where the school is, he explains to the boy that if he works hard he will become a chain-man for the Survey of India; in other words, play the hidden Game. Kim understands, and thinks that it is a good idea because it will allow him to take to the Road again on his wanderings. The lama appears outside the school to watch Kim go up to the 'Gates of Learning'. He tells Kim that he must go back to Benares to stay in the Temple of the Tirthankars, until it is time for him to find the River. He hopes to have Kim as his disciple again on the Search, but, for now, Kim must 'acquire wisdom'.

Kim learns much at St Xavier's, but he runs back to the Road each holiday. The first time he does so like a polo-pony, breaking loose to learn the Game alone. He goes freely among the people, making friends everywhere. Then he joins Mahbub again, and, while sleeping near his men as the new horse-boy, overhears two men disguised as fakirs plotting to kill Mahbub. Kim warns Mahbub and so saves his life. Then he goes up to Simla with the Pathan and his horses, for Kim is to stay here for the rest of the holiday. Here Kim is learning all the time from the owner of the house, Lurgan Sahib, 'the healer of sick pearls'. Apart from doctoring precious stones, Lurgan gives Kim insight into magic and the occult, trains his memory, and lets him practise to perfection the art of changing disguises. Here, too, he meets the Bengali babu, Hurree Chunder Mookerjee, who takes him back to St Xavier's and, on the way, encourages him to learn all about measuring distances, and to use drugs, like quinine, in case of sickness.

Several times in the next three years, the lama turns up in Lucknow to visit Kim, and in each holiday Kim goes out adventuring with Mahbub, or learns more at Lurgan's. By the time he is sixteen, Mahbub begs Colonel Creighton to let the boy go out with the Red Lama for six months, to run free, learning all the time. So Kim's schooling is finished. Protected by the sorceress Huneefa's ritual, he sets out as a Son of the Charm, one of a secret service.

He collects his holy man from Benares and they travel north. While on the train, Kim saves the life of another agent, E.23. Although Kim is pleased with this achievement, the lama chides him for his pride and for having acted when he could not see what the consequences of his action would be. Yet the lama feels that his Search is sure, now he has his disciple back again.

Near the hills of the north, they stay with the old Kulu woman at Saharunpore. The sahiba tells them she has a doctor in the household, and this turns out to be none other than the babu. He compliments Kim on his success in saving their mutual friend, E.23, and then tells him that he is to meet two Russian spies who are in league with the Five Kings, and plan to make all ready for an army to come through the passes. The babu asks for Kim's assistance when he contacts the spies, who are mapping in the hills. Kim and the babu persuade the lama to walk into the hills for a while, saying that his River will break forth at his feet, wherever he goes. The babu travels ahead of Kim and the lama, still in his doctor's, or *hakim's,* disguise, until he catches up with the strange sahibs, and appears to them as an agent for a rajah, who has been sent to assist them. They have maps and papers and a *murasla* (king's letter) in their baggage.

They accept the babu's services, and he takes charge of their coolies, leading them all towards Simla. The party meet the lama and his *chela* while the lama is expounding the Way to Kim, using a chart of the Wheel of Life which he has drawn himself. The Russian tries to buy it; when the lama will not sell, he rips it and strikes the lama in the face. The coolies snatch up the stunned lama and make off with all the guns and baggage. Kim attacks the Russian and then runs off, too, to take charge of the baggage while the babu remains with the spies. The lama prevents the coolies, who are Buddhist, from avenging his injury, and they go to Shamlegh-under-the-Snows to share out their booty. Kim keeps the valuable documents and discards the rest of the basket over Shamlegh-midden. The Woman of Shamlegh loves Kim, and delivers a message for him to the babu. Then, when the old man is ill but, none the less, is desperate to return to the plains, she lends them a litter in which the lama is carried down and away from his beloved hills. Only a corner of his chart of Life remains untorn, and he must find the River soon. Kim is in need of rest, but supports his master all the way back to Saharunpore, as his faithful *chela*.

Kim collapses with exhaustion and fever, but is nursed by the sahiba. As soon as he is well she tells him that the same *hakim* is back again. Kim is much relieved to pass over the papers into the babu's keeping. The babu tells him that Mahbub is in the vicinity selling horses and that the lama has walked into a brook and says he is transfigured. Kim falls into a restoring sleep upon the earth, below a young banyan tree. Mahbub Ali and the lama see him and come up to talk about him while he sleeps. Mahbub will take Kim with him to the north in six months, for he is needed by the state. Meanwhile, he leaves him with the lama. When Kim wakes the lama explains to him how he has contemplated and achieved union with the Great Soul and has won deliverance for his *chela* too.

Detailed summaries

Chapter I

The tale begins with Kim sitting astride the gun Zam-Zammah. Kim had won his seat from a native boy, but this, we are told, is just 'since the English held the Punjab' and Kim is English (or, rather, of Irish parents, who are both dead). The orphan boy has grown up to be the 'Little Friend of all the World'. Everyone in Lahore seems to know him, from his playmates to the policeman, the water-carrier, and the young men for whom he goes on 'commissions – by night on the crowded house-tops'. He is 'lithe and inconspicuous' and loves to change his clothes to appear like a Hindu or Mohammedan boy.

Kim is fascinated by someone new, a man such as he has never seen before. This is a Tibetan lama who has come to Lahore to visit the museum. The lama and the curator of the museum talk together as fellow-craftsmen and scholars, and Kim, listening, decides to join the lama on his Search for the River where Buddha's arrow fell. The old man, who seems an innocent abroad, accepts Kim as his *chela,* and

Kim begins the occupation of disciple by begging food for his master, and a place to sleep in the Kashmir Serai, where he is friendly with a big Afghan horse-trader, Mahbub Ali.

Mahbub Ali is actually a secret agent of the government and entrusts a vital message into Kim's keeping, since he thinks that the boy is sure to be able to deliver it. Kim has a good idea of how dangerous it is to carry that report 'of a white stallion's pedigree' when he sees a man searching Mahbub's baggage with a knife. He wakes the lama and they leave immediately.

COMMENTARY: This is the starting-point for Kim and his travels, and in this chapter we are given both the vital threads of the whole story: the Search, or the contemplative side of man's nature, is indicated by the person of the lama, while the Game, the active part of life, is shown to us when Mahbub Ali appears. It is a sign of the abundant vitality with which Kim is endowed, that on the very same day he has decided to follow the Search with the lama, he also enters upon the Game with Mahbub's assistance.

Kim might seem to be only a waif whose father died taking opium, leaving him a white man's birth certificate and a prophecy concerning a Red Bull, an orphan whom missionaries ought to have looked after. But we soon learn that it is Kim's own views which make him avoid 'missionaries and white men of serious aspect'. Whatever he does, Kim does with verve. He gets his seat on the gun by kicking a Hindu boy off first; an accurate picture of any childhood. And this is no racial discrimination, for Kim himself is sun-burnt 'black', and speaks the vernacular language, just one among the many small boys of the bazaar. 'For Kim did nothing with an immense success.' He knows the whole of the old walled city, and 'he lived in a life wild as that of the Arabian nights'. He knows the young men of fashion and the holy fakirs too, and he is as clever as an actor in changing from one set of clothes into another. His is a theatrical life, full of intrigue on the roof-tops, of slipping 'into Hindu or Mohammedan garb'. Yet we are invited to consider Kim, not as an impudent ragamuffin, but as a boy who delights in life itself: 'what he loved was the Game for its own sake'. This, of course, is the essence of boyhood, when action itself is a pleasure, but it also shows us that Kim is an expert, a craftsman, in his own way, while absorbed in doing things he enjoys.

The other boys fear the foreign priest: Kim befriends him. The lama is an unworldly man: Kim chooses to travel through the world with him. He cannot comprehend the lama's beliefs, yet he can beg for him successfully, as he shows when he drives off the free-roaming Brahmini bull from the Hindu shopkeeper's stall, receiving a meal in return. He is proud of, and enjoys, his new responsibility.

When Kim suggests that perhaps, some day, he'll be made a king, the lama replies firmly 'I will teach thee other and better desires upon the road'. Immediately after this, they go to the Kashmir Serai, where Kim helps the horse-trader Mahbub Ali with his concerns. Now worldly ambitions come into play once more, for Kim is to run the risk of taking a secret message for Mahbub to Umballa, along the lama's way to Benares. The austere simplicity of the lama's manner of speaking contrasts strongly with the quick-thinking exchange between Mahbub and Kim. As yet, Kim does not know that Mahbub Ali is a secret agent as well as a horse-dealer. And Mahbub Ali is taking a great chance in sending Kim.

That same night, Mahbub goes off to drink perfumed brandy with the 'Flower of Delight'. His bunch of keys is stolen, and Kim sees 'a sleek young gentleman from Delhi' searching all Mahbub's possessions. Now that Kim is fully aware of the importance of what he carries, he acts decisively, and leaves for Umballa.

NOTES AND GLOSSARY:

loot:	plunder or pillage
fakirs:	holy men, Hindu devotees or naked ascetics
ghi:	boiled butter
bazar:	the permanent market or street of shops
būts:	idols
Sahib:	term of respect for Europeans, 'Sir'
būt-parast:	idolater, one who worships idols
stupa:	ancient Buddhist monument in the form of a solid dome
vihara:	Buddhist temple, originally the hall where the monks met
dewas:	gods
Bodhisat:	the Lord Buddha
chela:	faithful disciple, follower or pupil
bilaur:	crystal
kunjri:	low-caste vegetable seller
yogi:	a Hindu ascetic
yagi:	bad-tempered
bhisti:	water-bearer
pardesi:	foreigner
serai:	building for the accommodation of travellers and their animals; enclosed yard
hookah:	Indian pipe for smoking through water; hubble-bubble
maharaj:	great king
pundit:	a learned man

| kafila: | a body or convoy of travellers; caravan |
| choor: | thief |

Chapter II

The lama, made nervous in the railway station, is guided by Kim, who buys one ticket to Umballa, and another to Amritzar.

They climb aboard a crowded third-class carriage. The occupants of this carriage are a Hindu Jat cultivator and his wife, a young soldier of a Sikh regiment, an Amritzar courtesan, a Sikh craftsman, and a fat Hindu moneylender.

At Amritzar, the ticket-collector tells Kim to get out. The lama does not understand why Kim is not to be allowed to go with him. On the platform, Kim begs ticket money from the courtesan, and the lama blesses the girl in Tibetan.

They travel on, seeing all the rich Punjab, making their morning meal, and hearing the tale of the Buddha's arrow from the lama, who says his prayers and meditates over his beads. The 'gentle, tolerant folk,' Kipling says, 'looked on reverently'. Kim tells them of his own search for the Red Bull.

At Umballa, the cultivator and his wife invite them to stay in the courtyard of their relative's house. Kim leaves the lama safely there, and steals out to deliver his secret message. He finds the Englishman's house and, unseen, passes the note to him. Then Kim stays on to see what will happen next. He hears the conversation between his man and a stranger who turns out to be the Commander-in-Chief. The upshot of the message is that eight thousand troops are to be mobilised.

Back with his hosts, Kim enjoys a theological discussion between the family priest and his lama. The Brahmin casts Kim's horoscope, and foretells that Kim will find his Bull within three days, and that his is a Sign of War.

Kim and the lama depart in the dawn.

COMMENTARY: This chapter colours in the realism of Kipling's sketches of India and her characters. Aspects of Kim's nature, too, are filled in for us. For example, he is more cunning than the railway clerk who would have cheated them by giving a ticket for the nearest station. Kim is amazed at the lama's 'immense simplicity'; he obviously needs his disciple.

Their fellow-passengers are all minor characters who become familiar to us in the space of less than a chapter. The 'well-to-do cultivator' is a blue-turbaned Hindu, who smokes an acrid pipe and has a garrulous wife. He is conjured up for us by a physical description, when he shrugs 'one knotted, bronzed shoulder'.

The moneylender's meanness is *his* characteristic, when he begs the guard to be merciful to Kim, yet does not offer money to help him. In contrast, the Amritzar courtesan is generous, and the lama, in his confusion, says of her, 'Beyond doubt it was a nun'. The moneylender laughs at the lama's simplicity, remarking 'There be ten thousand such nuns in Amritzar alone'.

As the train speeds along, 'All the rich Punjab lay out in the splendour of the keen sun', while in the compartment the lama is telling the tale of the Lord Buddha to these gentle, kindly folk. They understand him because 'All India is full of holy men, stammering gospels in strange tongues'; and meanwhile Kim spits red *pan*-juice on the floor. He revels in native habits; 'the boy was entirely happy to be out chewing *pan* and seeing new people in the great good-tempered world'.

Tired at the end of the day, they are immediately given accommodation by relatives of the cultivator and his wife. This is the famous hospitality of the people. Yet the lama regrets how far he has come from his monastery, saying 'Alas! It is a great and terrible world'.

Kim does not think so, for he 'stole away, as unremarkable a figure as ever carried his own and a few score thousand other folk's fate slung round his neck'. His is the life of action, in contrast to the thoughtful life of the lama.

Kim shows himself to be ideal for his new trade when he delivers the message, and also stays there to see what result will come of it.

From present and coming events of war, we are returned to the calm, age-old traditions of India, when the two tolerant old priests engage in theological discussion. Tolerance is the flower of both their creeds, the Brahmin's and the lama's. Casting horoscopes, they are in the courtyard 'pointing upwards as the big stars sailed across the dark'. The priest draws Kim's horoscope in the dust with a twig, and his predictions are surprisingly accurate. They confirm Kim's sense of pride in his destiny, but the lama's main worry is whether he will overpass the River in his travels. The customs and the credibility of Indian beliefs in astrology are well established by this and the following chapter.

NOTES AND GLOSSARY:

Jat:	agricultural race of north-west India
naik:	corporal
pulton:	battalion, a regiment of native infantry
tikkut:	ticket
pan:	betel leaf wrapped around areca nut and a smear of lime, to be chewed
Dogra	a Punjabi tribe

Chapter III

The lama and his disciple walk across the fields looking for the River. They are surprised by the appearance of a cobra. Kim wants to find a stick and break its back, but the lama commands 'Let him live out his life' and speaks to the snake as his brother.

At evening they rest in a village, on 'the brickwork plinth under the great tree'. The headman sends for the priest to interpret the lama's tale, and the priest advises them to follow the Grand Trunk Road which runs nearby, since it overpasses every stream on this side of India.

Kim, enjoying the village audience, prophesies war, and wins the admiration of an old soldier who recognises the Commander-in-Chief from Kim's impersonation. Kim stays with the old soldier for the night, and the lama goes with the priest – but not before Kim has taken their purse to keep it safe.

In the morning the old rissaldar (the native officer who commanded in a cavalry regiment), on his pony, leads them on their way to the road. He tells tales of the days of the Mutiny, in which he was loyal to the British. He says how he longs to have his former strength back again.

In reply, the lama àdvises him to enter the Way which is the path to freedom, and they sit in the shade of a mango tree while the lama explains the Law. Both old men fall asleep, and are wakened by a little child. The lama ignores the child at first, then gives it his rosary beads to play with, and sings it a song.

The rissaldar sings them the song of Nikal Seyn [Nicholson], and they reach the Grand Trunk Road. Here they meet one of the old soldier's sons, also a rissaldar, a wild rider chasing a carter who has frightened his young mare.

COMMENTARY: Here again our notion of the lama is enlarged, as, first, he warns Kim against pride, when Kim has bested a market-gardener who was rude to them. And then, when Kim dreads the cobra and wants to thrash it to death with a stick, the lama tells him to let it live, saying to the cobra, 'May thy release come soon, brother!' and asking it if it knows the whereabouts of his River. He walks beside it without harm, though Kim is in a sweat of fear. Then he commands Kim to follow. Kim obeys, which shows how implicitly he trusts his master.

The picture of the village is a study in naturalism: the crops are named, the village dogs are roused, the travellers are offered a place in the shade, milk and a meal. Every Indian village has its tree, its brickwork plinth, mud walls, a string bedstead for the visitor. The

cattle are coming in from the grazing grounds, the women are pre-
paring the evening meal, the prayers are finished in the temple, as the
lama and Kim tell their tales to their audience.

Kim is motivated by a desire to feel important as he impresses
the villagers, and especially the old soldier, with his prophecy. At the
same time he is cunning enough to save their purse from being taken
by the greedy priest.

The old soldier accompanies them in the morning and gives them the
story of his life. The lama responds by explaining his Way. Both old
men fall asleep despite expounding and listening to the Most Excellent
Law. This is a humorous moment, given point by the small child who,
making its obeisance before the holy man, falls over and cries. The
lama lets it play with his beads and comforts it with a song. At this, the
old rissaldar remarks, '. . . he has made a child happy. There was a
very good householder lost in thee, my brother'.

We are made aware of the historical setting when the rissaldar
harks back to past events and sings the song of Nikal Seyn before
Delhi. In this way men remember India's past.

They reach the great road which is like a river of all castes and kinds
of men. Here they meet one of the rissaldar's unruly sons, himself
grey-bearded, cracking his whip in chase of a carter, and riding a
'thin, high Kathiawar mare with eyes and nostrils aflame', who
'rocketed out of the jam, snorting and wincing as her rider bent her
across the road in chase . . .'. The old man proudly acknowledges
his child 'and they embraced as do father and son in the East'.

NOTES AND GLOSSARY:

mali:	gardener
būt:	a spirit
top-khana:	cannon – department, artillery
jaghir:	hereditary land-holding
rissaldar:	captain of a cavalry regiment
mango tope:	mango grove or orchard
koss:	a distance of about two miles
Chumar:	leatherworkers' caste
bunnia:	grain-seller

Chapter IV

The rissaldar's son confirms that there is to be a war. Father and
son go home, giving Kim a coin, of which a constable tries to cheat
him. Kim outwits the policeman, and says to the lama how well he
guards him as his disciple. The lama replies, 'I consider in my own
mind whether thou art a spirit, sometimes, or sometimes an evil imp'.

As they walk the 'broad, smiling river of life' which is the Grand Trunk Road, the lama is deep in meditation, noticing nothing, while Kim delights in the 'new people and new sights at every stride'.

At evening they stop at a *parao* or resting-place, where they join the retinue of an old lady who is the widow of a hill rajah. Being from the hills, she is in awe of the lama, and wishes him to accompany her procession as her priest.

COMMENTARY: This chapter is rich in description. Kim is gaining new experience of life, and of people, along the road, while in contrast the lama withdraws into contemplation and sees nothing, neither the newly released prisoner, nor the wild Sikh devotee, nor the villagers going to a local fair, nor the marriage procession, nor the jugglers.

The Grand Trunk Road is 'a stately corridor . . . all India spread out to left and right', and Kim finds it 'beautiful to watch the people, little clumps of red and blue and pink and white and saffron, turning aside to go to their own villages, dispersing and growing small by twos and threes across the level plain'. Kim feels the beauty of these things, and in the midst of them he walks along, spitting out the pith of sugar-cane.

By the time they reach the resting-place, 'the sun was driving broad golden spokes through the lower branches of the mango-trees'; says Kipling, lighting the scene for us. 'Swiftly the light gathered itself together, painted for an instant the faces and the cart-wheels and the bullocks' horns as red as blood. Then the night fell . . .'

If the first part of this chapter concerns itself with description, the second is largely composed of witty conversations and explanations concerning the old lady whom they have the good luck to meet. The exchanges of wit between Kim and the old lady are especially good. Kim thinks of her as 'an old lady of charming manners and infinite resource'. He is proud to be travelling with her and her escort as well as his lama, '. . . this was life as he would have it . . . India was awake, and Kim was in the middle of it, more awake and more excited than anyone . . .' The infinite variety of India is ours to enjoy through the medium of Kim, who takes such delight in it all.

NOTES AND GLOSSARY:

takkus:	tax
Sirkar:	the government
belaitee-pani:	English water, soda-water
Sansi:	an untouchable
Akali:	Sikh zealot
Khalsa:	Sikh religion
changars:	railway-working caste, whose women work

puttees:	leggings, gaiters made from a strip of cloth
parao:	resting-place
ruth:	carriage drawn by oxen, used by women on journeys
Oorya:	Orissa farming caste
pahari:	hillman
zemindar:	landholder
shraddha:	offering for a dead person
sitar:	stringed instrument of India
gâli:	abuse
zenana:	secluded women's apartments
nut-cut:	rogue

Chapter V

Reaching their next halt an hour before sundown, Kim takes a walk across country with the lama. They sit in a mango grove, and suddenly white soldiers appear, marking out a camp. The first two soldiers set up the crest of their regiment, a Red Bull, fulfilling the prophecy concerning Kim.

At nightfall the whole regiment appears and pitches camp. Kim leaves the lama hidden nearby and crawls up to the mess-tent door, where he sees the sahibs drink a toast to the Bull. The chaplain, Mr Bennett, comes out of the tent abruptly, treads on Kim, struggles with and captures him. He takes the boy to his tent to question him. There the chaplain finds the amulet and Kim is surprised into speaking English. Father Victor, the Roman Catholic chaplain, helps by reading Kim's papers and remembering his father, Kimball O'Hara. Kim tells some of the story of his life, ending by telling them he is a disciple, and fetching in the Holy One to prove he is no thief.

The clergymen tell them that Kim must stay with the regiment and be sent to a school. The lama is distressed by their taking his disciple from him, but he asks of Father Victor the price of the best schooling a boy can get in India, and leaves.

Kim has every intention of escaping and running back to his lama. Meanwhile, he impresses the padres and the colonel and soldiers by foretelling that they will go to the 'new War'.

COMMENTARY: Kim and the lama watch in astonishment as the soldiers plant the camp-marking flag 'snap-snapping in the evening breeze not ten feet away'. It is Kim's Sign, sure enough, that has appeared right in front of them; 'the device that flamed like a ruby in the dusk' seems like a vision to Kim, but the lama corrects him, saying 'But this is not vision. It is the world's Illusion, and no more'. They wait, and see

the regiment pitch camp. Later, Kim creeps back, having left the lama
in a hollow, for he suspects that night will be the time that the sahibs
might pray to the Bull. 'Kim's limitations were as curious and sudden as
his expansions', we are told, and sure enough, he seems to be seeing the
sahibs praying when they hold out their glasses to the Bull. A moment
afterwards he is Bennett's prisoner. Bennett is not a sympathetic
man, and it takes Father Victor to make sense of Kim's papers and his
story. Kim relates the Umballa horoscope and his father's sayings to
them. Bennett thinks he is 'a phenomenal little liar', but Father Victor
knows it is O'Hara's boy and says that the holy man must be invited in.

Kim describes the Englishmen to the lama in the vernacular, since
they cannot talk Hindu, as 'donkeys'. But the lama checks him, saying,
'Then it is not well to make a jest of their ignorance'. The lama does
not receive similar courtesy from the white men, for Bennett
considers him only a 'heathen' and speaks of him as 'this *fakir*'. Yet
Father Victor has sympathy for the lama when he hears the story of his
Search and understands his sorrow at parting from Kim. As soon as the
lama knows that Kim is the son of a sahib, he says that Kim must do as
all other white men do. How will he find his River without his
disciple? He does not know, yet his real concern is for Kim: 'You
take him from me and you cannot say what you will make him'. He
realises that the more money is paid, in the white men's world, the
better education is given, and he finds out Father Victor's address, and
leaves.

Kim knows that 'Sooner or later, if he chose, he could escape into
great, grey, formless India', the India he knows better than any padres
or soldiers could. He enjoys impressing them by prophesying war, and
feels confident as a superior sort of white man, with his omniscient
point of view.

NOTES AND GLOSSARY:

ferashes:	servants in charge of tents
Mallum?:	do you understand?
kabarri:	second-hand dealer
madrissah:	school
Kismet:	fate
Gorah-log:	white people

Chapter VI

In the morning Kim's prophecy is proved true. The Mavericks march
to Umballa, and take trains to the Front. Kim is left behind with a
drummer-boy in charge of him, and with a schoolmaster who forces
him into the schoolroom. He determines to escape somehow. Although

he is not allowed to go near the bazaar, he sends a sweeper to fetch him a letter-writer, and writes to Mahbub Ali asking him for help. Back in barracks, Father Victor tells him that the lama has written offering to pay the three hundred rupees a year for the boy's education in St Xavier's school.

Kim has to spend the next three days with the other boys in barracks, which he loathes. But the drummer-boy who beats him is beaten in his turn when Mahbub Ali arrives and gallops off with Kim on to the Umballa racecourse. There they meet the same sahib to whom Kim had delivered the letter concerning the pedigree of a white stallion, Colonel Creighton. Mahbub explains something of Kim's background to the colonel, and they take Kim back to the padre. Kim has caught the colonel's interest. Creighton recommends Father Victor to accept the note of hand that the lama has sent, and says that he himself will see the boy down to Lucknow, where the school is. Kim will be under his protection from now on.

COMMENTARY: Kim's fate takes a new turn in this chapter. He hates the idea of being confined to school, having spent his life avoiding discipline. Using his wits, he surprises the sweeper by his knowledge of abusive language, and orders him to fetch the letter-writer, who is trapped into writing the letter to Mahbub Ali without payment because of his curiosity to know more about this 'white boy who is not a white boy'.

Father Victor has to ask Kim's advice over the matter of the lama's letter. This letter contains the lama's opinion that 'Education is greatest blessing if of best sorts. Otherwise no earthly use'. This is why he is sending the money for the boy 'who is apple of eye'. Kim is quite sure that, if the lama has promised to send three hundred rupees every year, he will send them.

Meantime, Kim has to endure the drummer-boy's beatings and abuse, though he enjoys hearing the servants call the boy names to his face which he does not understand. All in all, Kim has a working knowledge of people which both padre and drummer-boy lack. What use will he make of it, we wonder?

This is a question Mahbub Ali has obviously been asking himself, for while he seems unlikely to help Kim escape from the English, he tells Colonel Creighton all about him, in a manner that will catch the colonel's attention: 'He was born in the land . . . He goes where he chooses . . . He is . . . a sharp chap . . . in a twinkling he would be a low-caste Hindu boy . . . They will send him to a school . . . Then he will forget all he knows . . . I sent him to deliver a message once . . . .' These are vital details to the colonel, who decides to take Kim under his wing for the purposes of the Game, saying to Mahbub that 'the colt will be entered for polo only'. In other words, Kim is a born agent, and is too good to be wasted. The colonel persuades Kim not to run away after all, by promising that he will go with him to Lucknow, 'seeing and hearing new things all the while'. This shows how he appreciates Kim's nature, and understands what matters to him most.

NOTES AND GLOSSARY:

Kayeth:	writer caste
chabuk sawai:	a sharp chap
pie:	a small coin
hoondi:	a note of hand, from a native banker
Nucklao:	Lucknow

Chapter VII

Kim writes another letter, this time to his Holy One at Benares, begging him to come to Lucknow to see him at the new school. He inquires of the letter-writer who Colonel Creighton is, and is told that he has no regiment, is a fool easily cheated about horses, and is interested in the customs of the people. Kim knows he is no fool, and so must be playing a hidden game.

Kim goes south on the train and the colonel instructs him about his future on the journey. At Lucknow Kim orders his driver to take him round the city before going to the school. He admires Lucknow very much, and then, outside the school wall, he sees his lama, who has come to see him 'going up into the Gates of Learning'. The lama insists that he does not come because of affection for Kim, but to help him to wisdom. Kim begs him not to go away for good, saying he is all alone in the world but for him. The lama says he will return from time to time. He watches Kim go through the gates, and goes back to Benares.

In St Xavier's, Kim learns much among the other boys, all of whom are 'country born and bred'. But when the holidays come he is determined not to be sent to a barrack-school, and wanders off on his own, 'in the likeness of a low-caste Hindu boy'. He takes to the Road again, but eventually turns up to meet Mahbub Ali. Mahbub and the colonel have already decided that Kim is learning the game and perfecting his knowledge of the land in his own way, so he goes on to Umballa with Mahbub.

COMMENTARY: Kim is learning the trade the colonel follows, and which he himself will follow. The colonel is a man after Kim's own heart, 'a tortuous and indirect person playing a hidden game'. Travelling to Lucknow in a solitary carriage, Kim begins to think, 'Who is Kim?' 'He considered his own identity, a thing he had never done before, until his head swam'. Sent for by the colonel who tells him he will enter the Survey of India as a chain-man, and speaks to him in fluent Urdu, Kim decides that this is a good idea, since it will allow him to return to the Road again. He respects the colonel, 'whose eyes were so different from the dull fat eyes of other sahibs'.

Kim shows both self-possession and a spirited nature in conversation with the colonel, and lets the colonel's advice 'not to despise the black men' sink into his heart.

His conversation with the lama in Lucknow is quite different. He prostrates himself at the lama's feet, as a true disciple. Kim is without any reserve in his love of the lama, whom he trusts more than anyone else. But the lama shies away from the 'Red Mist' of affection, saying he came to see Kim set on the path of learning. Kim says that surely it was to see him he came. The lama admits that he will come to see him from time to time, and hopes, if Kim is to be a sahib, he will be one like the curator of the museum in Lahore, who was 'wiser than many abbots'. Kim cries passionately, 'If I eat thy bread, how shall I ever forget thee?', referring to the fact that the lama is paying for his education. He is 'clutching at the robe, all forgetful that he was a Sahib'. And the lama too is moved: 'Let me see thee go . . . . Dost thou love me? Then go, or my heart cracks . . . .'

The 'self-reliant' boys of St Xavier's are described. They come from all over India, and have all had adventures. Kim learns to read and write, and after his hard work, decides to roam off on his own in the holidays. First, he disguises himself in Lucknow, at a house of disreputable women, pretending he is in love with a girl whom he must get to see secretly. He takes the train to Umballa in his new disguise; 'In all India that night was no human being so joyful as Kim'.

Mahbub and Colonel Creighton discuss his disappearance at Simla. They decide it is all for the good that he learns to go alone, since 'When he comes to the Great Game he must go alone – alone, and at peril of his head. Then, if he spits, or sneezes, or sits down other than as the people do whom he watches, he may be slain.' They won't hinder him in his adventure, but next time he must go with Mahbub. Kim turns up unexpectedly, 'the little drenched figure dancing in the wet' and tells Mahbub what adventures he has had. Mahbub is much impressed: 'Shabash!' (Well done!) he says to Kim.

NOTES AND GLOSSARY:

ticca-gharri:	four-wheeled carriage for hire
naikan:	dancing-girl
Hubshi:	Negro, or one with short curly hair
Shaitan:	the Evil One, Satan

teli:	oilman
rêl:	railway
Shabash!:	well done!

Chapter VIII

Kim changes his clothing for that of a Mohammedan boy, to go with Mahbub. They agree that their lives lie in one another's hands, and Kim, unlike a sahib, says he 'made a fault' to think that the Pathan betrayed him by handing him back to the English at Umballa. 'I say now, Hajji, that it was well done; and I see my road all clear before me to a good service.'

Kim goes to sleep with Mahbub's followers and horses, while Mahbub stays in the city. Half-asleep, he hears whispering from behind a horse-truck, where two men disguised as fakirs lie in wait to murder Mahbub when he rides in. Kim steals away and warns Mahbub on the road.

Mahbub makes use of his knowledge of Englishmen to tell a young sahib on the railway that he suspects thieves at his horse-trucks. The enthusiastic superintendent takes a light engine down the line, and he and a policeman fight with the fakirs and arrest them.

Kim and Mahbub take the horses to Simla, where Kim, disguised as a Eurasian lad, is to lodge with Lurgan Sahib.

COMMENTARY: In conversation with Mahbub, Kim shows how he knows and loves the land. He also shows how well he understands Mahbub's and the Colonel's business, and Mahbub admires his knowingness, 'And with these things on thy mind, dost thou lie down and rise again among all the sahibs' little sons at the *madrissah* and meekly take instruction from thy teachers?' Kim and he agree that Kim will return to the school, but Kim says, 'when the *madrissah* is shut, then must I be free and go among my people. Otherwise I die!' When Mahbub asks him who his people are, Kim replies 'This great and beautiful land'. The land and its people are as one, to him. Later, in camp with Mahbub's horse-boys, Kim is 'utterly happy' with his new change of scene. He feels very old and wise. He is quick to act, to save Mahbub from the fakirs, and we appreciate Mahbub's cunning, he who knows the sahibs so well he can use them for his own ploy, when his enemies are arrested by them.

Kim travels the road to Simla 'in the fresh of the rainswept dawn' with Mahbub, and Kim insists that it is to the lama that his heart is drawn, and that he is bound to rejoin him on his Search some day.

Meanwhile, Kim is to stay in Lurgan Sahib's shop and learn all that he can, obeying Lurgan in everything.

NOTES AND GLOSSARY:

Hajji:	one who has accomplished his pilgrimage to Mecca
Pathan:	an Afghan
Eblis:	the Devil
bhang:	a drug from hemp
Jehannum:	Hell
Narain!:	an exclamation used by Hindus
churel:	ghost of a woman who has died in childbirth. Her feet point backwards
Sunni:	Mohammedan sect
mehteranee:	sweeper woman
bhungi:	sweeper, scavenger
Allah kerim!:	Allah have mercy!
tonga:	two-wheeled cart drawn by a pony, for hire
jhampanis:	rickshaw coolies, men who pulled rickshaws

Chapter IX

Kim is led to Mr Lurgan's house by a Hindu child about ten years old, who turns out to be Lurgan's own servant. The house is full of such things as devil-dance masks, scented oils, sandalwood incense and Asian weapons. In the midst of it, Lurgan sits at a table stringing pearls. He leaves Kim to spend a restless night in the room full of curiosities, strange voices and music. Kim finds and jams the phonograph, then sleeps.

In the morning he has a good look at Lurgan, who dresses as a sahib, but seems to be an Asiatic, keeping a shop full of wonders. He heals sick pearls, he says, but he also works magic. He can make a heavy clay water-jug cross the room to Kim. Later, when the jug is smashed, he puts his hand on the back of Kim's neck and asks him if he can see the jug coming into shape again. Kim, however, concentrates on the multiplication table, and does not let Lurgan make him see the jug form again. Lurgan is very impressed, saying Kim is the first person to resist the idea that it could form again. But Kim does not tell him how he controlled his mind.

The jealous little Hindu child, who has tried to kill Lurgan before breakfast because he thinks his master is fond of the new boy, shows Kim the Play of the Jewels. They also practise this memory game with common odds and ends on a tray. This is Kim's new school, where he also perfects his art of dressing-up.

A babu arrives who finds Kim's performance efficient. He is Kim's companion on the way back to St Xavier's. This Bengali, Hurree Chunder Mookerjee, also plays the secret Game for Colonel Creighton. The babu gives Kim a drug-box, and advises him to learn how to measure distances as best he can. This Kim applies himself to, back at St Xavier's.

Meanwhile, in Benares, the lama knows he will not find his River without the one *chela* who must search with him, and tells the priests of the temple a tale from the *Jâtaka* to illustrate his point.

COMMENTARY: Lurgan is said to work magic, and his first words to Kim, 'Do not be afraid', would suggest that some are afraid of his powers. Kim, however, does not allow himself to be cowed, either by his night-time experience of strange voices, or by the conjuring trick with the jug. He is not suggestible, in the sense that the supernatural power exerted by Lurgan cannot take over his mind. Lurgan is impressed by finding that there is no flaw in the jewel. Kim, for his part, is willing to learn anything he can at Lurgan's: notice his attempts to become expert at memorising the items seen briefly on the tray. Lurgan explains that such things are learnt 'By doing it many times over till it is done perfectly – for it is worth doing'.

Kim perfects the dressing-up game: he does this better than the little Hindu boy, because Kim's mind can 'temper itself to enter another's soul'. During these changes of speech and gesture he pretends to be a fakir, and for the first time meets the babu, whose opinion of Kim's performance leads him to ask 'How soon can he become approximately efficient chain-man?'

Kim envies even the fat babu, once he knows that he too has a letter and a number and a price upon his head. Kim understands the reasons why he must apply himself to mathematics and map-making and elementary surveying, and he does well in these at school over the next couple of years.

It is significant, here, that the lama indicates the course of the whole story by telling a *Jâtaka* tale, or parable of the Lord Buddha, to the priests in the temple. It is the one about the ringed elephant be-friending the young calf who grows up and breaks the ring. The *Jâtaka* tales themselves are the earliest story forms in Indian literature.

NOTES AND GLOSSARY:

khanda:	sword
kuttar:	dagger
Chûp!:	be quiet! Still!
Dekho!:	look!
Kubbee:	never
nahin:	no
ruttee:	a jeweller's weight of about a carat
vakil:	lawyer, attorney
Jâtaka:	book of the lives of Buddha

Chapter X

Each holiday either Lurgan or Mahbub Ali is busy finishing off Kim's education. Out with Mahbub to Bombay or Quetta, or crossing the desert sands, he learns how to make up reports and maps. From Lurgan he learns about charms and the use of drugs, among other things.

When Kim completes a written report of a remote area for the colonel, Mahbub gives him Pathan dress, and a small revolver. It is this report, too, which makes Colonel Creighton agree that Kim should go out on the Road again, with his Red Lama. He is to get experience for six months.

Kim is released from school to became an 'assistant chain-man'. He meets up with Mahbub, who engages a sorceress, Huneefa, to work magic spells for Kim's protection, and prepares him for the Road. Hurree Babu observes this spectacle and brings Kim's costume for the Road, that of a *chela*. He gives Kim a special amulet which is the mark of his being a Son of the Charm, one of the secret agents, along with a test-sentence which will help him recognise the others.

Hurree insists that if Kim were 'Asiatic' he would be employed right away, but these six months are to make him 'de-Englished' again.

Kim is ready to set off.

COMMENTARY: Kim understands more and more about different ways of life in India. With Mahbub, he is learning about specifically Muslim customs, especially those of the north-west, for example, when 'He dipped his hand into the dish with that great trader'. This refers to the Afghan custom at feasts when everyone takes their food from the same great central dish. Clearly Kim adapts to the habits of whatever race he is with.

He earns his keep, too, by obtaining information. All this he can only learn upon the Road, not at school. Mahbub treats him as his son, when he gives him the dress of honour and the revolver, showing how much he loves him.

Lurgan insists that the younger Kim is used at the Game, the better, and Colonel Creighton agrees that the boy has passed every examination. When Mahbub urges 'Let him out – let him go' and compares him to the polo-pony who is finished and whose rein must be dropped to let him go, the colonel agrees to let Kim take the Road, though not in any dangerous employment such as their business in the south.

So their pupil sets out, protected by Huneefa's ritual of calling up the devils. Hurree Babu also prepares him by giving him exact particulars about how to recognise another government agent on the road, and sending him out to forget the English side of his nature. He is to become as Asiatic as possible. This Kim happily does, feeling that it is 'rapture' to be in his *chela's* costume.

NOTES AND GLOSSARY:

lakh:	a hundred thousand of anything
pukka:	proper, right, thorough
dustoorie:	commission
salaams:	greetings
Jadoo:	magic
dawut:	invocation
Sufi:	free-thinker
hawa-dilli:	a heart-lifter, an amulet
tarkecan:	vegetable curry

Chapter XI

Kim travels alone to Benares. He is guided to the Temple of the Tirthankars by a Punjabi farmer, a Kamboh who is searching for a cure for his small son. They wait together for the lama to come out of the temple. Kim tries to heal the child with medicine from his drug-box, while the lama looks on. His master is impressed by this new role of physician.

They spend the night in the Jain temple, and set out for the north in the morning, along with the Kamboh, whose child is cured.

A Mahratta enters their compartment on the train. This man, by his amulet and his speech, Kim recognises as a fellow Son of the Charm. Cut and beaten, the Mahratta is in the midst of an adventure of the Great Game, for he has hidden a valuable letter under the Queen's Stone at Chitor, and is, even now, fleeing from his pursuers.

Kim disguises the Mahratta as a holy man, using ash and flour from the Kamboh's bundle. He makes the farmer promise to keep silent about the change he has seen. The lama too has seen Kim making a disguise for the Mahratta, and warns Kim against being too proud of his knowledge. The train arrives in Delhi.

COMMENTARY: Kim reacts to his new independence by feeling alone in the world. He repeats his name over and over again to himself. This kind of speculation is common among Asiatics, we are told. A Hindu holy man, passing by, reads his thoughts, and tells him to 'go in hope, little brother', on his Search.

By chance Kim meets a Kamboh farmer, who has searched the temples of Benares for a cure for his little son. Kim recognises fever and starvation as the child's illness, and when the lama comes out to observe them, he gives meat-lozenges and quinine tablets with suitable invocations. The lama is pleased to think of Kim as a healer, 'and all the loving old soul of him looked out through his narrow eyes'. Kim forgets his white blood as he stoops to touch his master's feet in the dust.

In the lama's cell Kim is shown the lama's art of writing pictures of the Wheel of Life. He is one of the three men in all the world who can both draw and expound the meaning of the Great Wheel. The lama tells the *Jâtaka* story of the elephant with the leg-iron to Kim, and ends by saying that their Search is sure. It doesn't matter where they go. 'If need be, the River will break from the ground before us.' The lama insists that the sahibs do not have all the knowledge in this world, and that night Kim 'dreamed in Hindustani, with never an English word'.

The Kamboh meets them at the start of their journey with gifts of food, in return for the health of his child. He goes north in the train with them, and it is from his bundle that Kim gets the stuffs to make a theatrical change of the Mahratta from frightened trader into opium-relaxed holy man. The Kamboh is in awe of Kim's wisdom, and even E.23, for this is who the 'Mahratta' is, asks him 'Art thou only a beginner?' to which Kim replies, 'But two days entered to the Game, brother'. Even as the lama and Kim set out on their Search, Kim becomes involved in the operations of the Game. It is his fate.

NOTES AND GLOSSARY:

bairagi:	holy man
Kamboh:	Punjabi farming caste
pahareen:	hillwoman
Bhotiyal:	Tibet
Jain:	Buddhist-like Hindu sect
hing:	asafoetida, strong-tasting and smelling Indian resin used in cooking
lathi:	staff or stick
doab:	land by the confluence of two rivers
Mahratta:	name of a famous Hindu warrior race
tar:	telegram
atta:	native flour
saddhu:	holy beggar

Chapter XII

E.23 escapes the men who hunt for him, by carrying off his role as the saddhu. Then Kim is surprised as E.23 blunders out of the carriage in front of a district superintendent of police, surrenders his ticket to him, and follows him off through the crowd. But as it turns out, this particular Englishman is also involved in the Game, and has gone to send a telegram for E.23 as to the whereabouts of the letter he hid under the Queen's Stone. Kim admires the saddhu for telling the news by pretending to curse the sahib. He says farewell to E.23, and hurries to his carriage.

The Kamboh has gone, frightened by the saddhu's falling into the hands of the police. The lama accuses Kim of pride and tells him that he cannot know the consequences of his actions.

At Saharunpore they leave the train, but they do not go straight to the Kulu woman's house. In order that Kim may receive instruction, and the lama meditate upon the Way, they wander among the villages and fruit-gardens. They go to the sahiba's house eventually, where they find a Bengali *hakim* who turns out to be Hurree Babu. Hurree congratulates Kim on saving the life of E.23. The department is pleased with him. But the babu is really there to ask Kim for his help in finding two Russian spies who are in the hills, map-making and being received by hill rajahs.

Kim decides to go to see these strangers, and to help the babu, who is, he says, very fearful. He and the babu separately persuade the lama to go into the hills. They give the talkative but kindly old lady a charm for her grandson and, loaded with her gifts of food, they set off for the lower hills.

COMMENTARY: Kim, full of pride after helping E.23 to escape, is told by the lama, 'Thou hast loosed an Act upon the world, and as a stone thrown into a pool so spread the consequences thou canst not tell how far'. Kim is wise enough to accept the lama's rebuke, even at the height of his latest success in the Game.

The pace of events slows down when the lama makes no haste to go to the sahiba's house, saying 'Wise men do not run about like chickens in the sun'. Their leisurely journey through the villages gives Kim time to appreciate the lama's character and to understand the nature of their Search better: '. . . he spoke of all his wanderings up and down Hind; till Kim, who had loved him without reason, now loved him for fifty good reasons'.

They arrive at the sahiba's house, and she speaks to them from inside her palanquin, as she had done years ago on the pilgrimage. The lama has, in the past, given her spells to cure her grandson, and she wants another of his charms. She tells them that there is a Bengali master of medicine in the household. Kim and the Bengali debate together, then the *hakim* reveals himself to be Hurree Babu. Kim knows he has not come just to congratulate him, and it turns out that the babu wants Kim to back him up, when he goes to affiliate himself to the camp of the spies. 'I am Bengali – a fearful man'. He assures

Kim 'It will be a great feather in your cap'. Kim is eager to go north, playing the Great Game.

Kim loves to listen to the old lady's talk of men and women, and we are told he is 'as interested in the life of this world as she soon to leave it'. By contrast, the lama sees himself and Kim as 'two Souls seeking escape'.

Hurree Babu has swayed the lama's intentions by saying that he should take the cool air of the Hills, and that the River will break forth at his feet.

NOTES AND GLOSSARY:

tum mut?:	are you drunk?
nickle-jao!:	clear off!
zoolum:	tyranny
polis:	police
siris:	acacia tree
mynah:	Indian talking bird, like a black and yellow starling
hakim:	an authority, a master
palanquin:	box-litter for travelling in, with poles borne by four or six men
sinà:	drug
arplan:	drug
chowkedar:	watchman
dooli:	litter
bukh:	babble, gossip
sepoy:	native soldier, disciplined and dressed in European style
coolie:	a hired labourer, or burden-carrier
pahar:	hill land, country

Chapter XIII

The lama walks the hills as only a hillman can, untiring. Kim, aching and limping, becomes fitter than he was in the plains. They meet the *hakim* again and again among the hills; Kim is to keep within sight of his umbrella when they find the 'sportsmen'. The babu finds the spies just after a storm. Their coolies, who threw down their loads, have been threatened with rifles by the sahibs and are hiding in the forest. The babu passes himself off as 'agent for the Rajah of Rampur', and persuades their coolies to come back. The strangers give the babu drink, and he pretends to be drunk and talks treasonably about English rule in India. The foreigners believe he hates the English, and accept him as their guide.

The babu keeps his eyes on a *kilta*, or conical basket, full of maps and documents. On the second day they come across the lama expounding his chart to his disciple at the roadside. The sahibs listen to the lama's doctrine while Hurree tells Kim where they keep their reports. The men want the lama's picture, but he refuses to sell it. The lama begins to fold up his chart when the Russian snatches at it and it tears. The Russian strikes the lama full on the face. Kim flies at his throat. The coolies flee at the sacrilege they have seen. The Frenchman runs towards the lama, but is driven back by stones thrown by the coolies, who snatch the lama away with them. The Frenchman fires at Kim, who has beaten his enemy, and Kim returns fire with Mahbub's revolver. Kim hurries off. The babu remains with the spies. Kim finds the coolies ready to go back with the guns and destroy the sahibs. The lama stops them, saying that there will be no killing.

They go to Shamlegh-under-the-Snows, a grazing centre of a few huts. The coolies say that Kim can have the big *kilta*, since it is full of wonderful things, and he can draw out their magic.

Down the hill the sahibs lie out without tents, food, guns or maps, with only the babu to guide them. They have lost everything.

COMMENTARY: The lama's old strength is restored to him among the hills, for he was a man bred among mountains. Kim finds it hard going to keep up with him. They frequently meet Hurree Babu on the Road, for he is determined to meet the foreign agents and find compromising evidence on them. The background to this journey is the marvellous hill-country, described with its high snows and cruel passes, its deodar forests and still valleys.

When the babu catches up with the strange sahibs, the moment is right for them to accept his services, for they have been having trouble controlling their baggage-coolies. They accept his story of who he is, but strike him across the wrist (which no Englishman would do) when he upsets a *kilta*. Of course the babu now has the information he wants, which is that their documents are still with them. The babu is too clever for them when they try to loosen his tongue with drink. He pretends to hate English rule in India, and they cast this up to him next day.

The coolies do not consider these sahibs to be proper, since they do not travel with a retinue. Their suspicions make them ready to flee, and they do so in horror when the lama is struck. The Russian's insolence in wanting to buy the chart for money is overtopped by his ignorance in striking a holy man. The coolies, ready to run back and shoot the sahibs, are stopped by the lama's command. The lama struggles to control his passions before he says that there must be no killing. He stands up proudly against the coolies, even though he was tempted to allow them to take revenge for him.

NOTES AND GLOSSARY:

betah: hill tribesman
shikarri: hunter, sportsman
kilta: conical basket
beegar: forced labour
murasla: king's letter
serow: antelope

Chapter XIV

The coolies, the lama and Kim travel by moonlight to Shamlegh. It is perched above a drop of two thousand feet to Shamlegh-midden, the world's end where no man has yet set foot.

Kim tends the lama, but the old man is greatly distressed by the blow and the response he felt because of it. He was angry, and he felt 'a lust to return evil'. Now that evil will continue to work to its end, and he must meditate what it means for them.

In the morning, a 'fair-coloured woman' gives Kim the heavy *kilta* which the coolies have left for him. She is the Woman of Shamlegh. Kim opens it and finds survey-instruments, maps, and correspondence which includes a *murasla,* or king's letter. He keeps the letters and handwritten books, and throws the compasses and other things down the hillside. He sends a message to the babu to let him know that he has the letters safely. The Woman of Shamlegh has taken a great liking to Kim, and she carries the message for him, then brings one back from the babu which tells Kim to return by the same road as the one by which he came.

Kim and the lama sit on the hillside with the people of Shamlegh. The lama blesses his hills. Kim urges him to wait in Shamlegh but the lama says he has become strong in the hills only to be proud and do evil. He recalls an old battle with the monks and says he has forgotten his Search. Only a tiny piece of his chart remains untorn, and he takes it as a sign that there is only a short span of life left to him.

Buddha's arrow fell in the plains: they must return there. The Woman of Shamlegh orders her men to carry the lama in a litter, since he is too weak to walk.

COMMENTARY: In Shamlegh they are perched above the whole world, 'This is the world's end', says the coolie above the cliff. Here the lama must meditate, despite the after-effects of the blow, on the meaning of events, for them. His logic leads him to believe that, despite having saved the sahibs, he did evil. He came into the hills and became strong only to do evil and forget the Search: 'A brawler and a swashbuckler upon the hillsides was I'. He is desperate to

leave for the plains and renew his Search. His farewell to his hills is
very affecting. 'He blessed them in detail – the great glaciers, the
naked rocks, the piled moraines and tumbled shale; dry upland,
hidden salt-lake, age-old timber and fruitful water-shot valley one
after the other, as a dying man blesses his folk; and Kim marvelled at
his passion.'

The Woman of Shamlegh, who once loved a sahib and wore
European clothes, recognises that there is something of the sahib in
Kim. For this reason, she helps him. Yet another person sees something
to love in Kim. And she does not treat him like a child, but like a man.

NOTES AND GLOSSARY:

khud:	steep hillside
chang:	barley-beer
sinen:	cymbals

Chapter XV

The babu guides the foreign agents, by circuitous routes, back to
Simla. He receives a testimonial from them, praising his helpfulness,
then makes the return journey to Shamlegh, to hear where Kim has
gone. He makes long marches to follow Kim and the lama.

They reach the plains by litter, and pay the hill-folk's wage. Kim
and the lama walk on alone, with all the burden of the old man, the
heavy bag, and the secret writings upon Kim. He nurses the lama,
but he is not well himself. Kim is full of reproaches for himself, but
the lama comforts him.

When they reach the sahiba's house, the old woman takes over Kim,
and cures him with drinks, massage, rest, and then good food. Once
Kim is better, he hears from the sahiba that the lama has been refusing
food, went roving through the fields and tumbled into a brook; he says
he is freed from all sin. The sahiba also tells him that the *hakim* is
back. The babu comes into Kim's room, and at last Kim is able to hand
over the maps and documents, to his great relief. The babu is delighted
to have the evidence of the kings' treason to put before the British
government. He tells Kim that it was he who pulled the lama out of the
brook. Also, the babu is responsible for asking Mahbub Ali's help to
find the papers, in case they were stolen from Kim, and Mahbub is
therefore in the district, selling horses. Then the babu goes off to catch
the train for Umballa, with the papers.

Kim goes outside, to enter the world again. Unnerved by his illness,
he lies down on the ground, sleeping to regain his strength.

The lama and Mahbub Ali come looking for him at evening. The
lama tells Mahbub that Kim is sure to enter Paradise. It does not

matter what he does in life; the end is sure. Mahbub, reassured that Kim will be entering government service within six months, leaves.

The lama wakes Kim and tells him how he has found the River of the Arrow 'here – even here!' He is free from all sin, and so is Kim.

COMMENTARY: We marvel at the hardihood of the babu in his long marches. This is not what was expected of him; he has become 'lean and weather-worn'. Kim, equally, is in a state which we have not seen before; he is tired and weary at heart. But what a disciple he is, even so! 'He begged in the dawn, set blankets for the lama's meditation, held the weary head on his lap through the noonday heats, fanning away the flies till his wrists ached, begged again in the evenings, and rubbed the lama's feet, who rewarded him with promise of Freedom – to-day, to-morrow, or, at furthest, the next day'. He feels, in his weakness, that he has still not taken enough care of the lama, but the lama insists that he has been living on Kim's strength. This seems true, for the boy is drained when they reach Saharunpore, and it takes all the old lady's skill to restore his health: 'the old eat the young daily', she remarks to the lama.

When Kim is rid of his lethargy, he is further helped by the babu's relieving him of the papers. The babu is of the opinion that the lama is suffering from 'infirmity of fits', and only the babu's prompt action of pulling him out saved him from drowning. Ever the man of action we now realise him to be, the babu leaves to put the papers into the right hands.

Kim's great moment, when he seized all the right papers, has been and gone already, like other acts in the Great Game. Now he wanders outside and lets the wheels of his being 'lock up anew on the world without' after his sickness.

While he sleeps, Mahbub and the lama, who are the two beings who love him the most, talk beside him. Mahbub is there to remind us that Kim must soon enter the Game again. The lama, whose time on earth is short, is there to assure Kim of 'Freedom from the Wheel of Things'. Mahbub, though remaining unimpressed by the lama's religion, understands his fondness for Kim, for he feels it too, as indeed half India considers him her son. He recognises that holiness beyond particular faiths which Kim has always known in the lama, and leaves them together till Kim is ready to return to the world.

Kim wakes to hear the lama's news. He sees his master 'outlined jet-black against the lemon-coloured drift of light'. Teshoo Lama's soul had united with the Great Soul during contemplation, but he returned for his *chela's* sake and found the river at his feet. Free from sin, his body was pulled from the river. Kim asks, 'Wast thou very wet?' He is glad the babu was there to pull him out. Like Mahbub,

Kim is never of the same faith as the lama, but loves and reveres him. And the lama is satisfied that he has won salvation for his beloved, not only for himself.

NOTES AND GLOSSARY:

chudder:	sheet worn as a mantle by women of north India
chit:	letter of reference
Jannatu l'Adn:	the Garden of Eden
Nibban:	Buddhist *nirvana* or heaven
Pushtu:	Afghan language
dacoity:	violent robbery
Allah kerim!:	Allah have mercy!

Part 3

Commentary

Structure and style

What is *Kim*? It does not seem to be an ordinary novel, since it is without a plot. Its form is modelled on that first great example set by Cervantes (1547–1616) when he wrote his *Don Quixote* (1605). It can be called a *picaresque* novel (from the Spanish 'picaro', meaning a rogue), for it tells a story through episodes on a journey. *Don Quixote* is its real ancestor.

We do not feel the presence of the author himself, but the unity of the book comes from Kim. The narrative style tells the tale of his adventures with interest and vitality, like Kim's own nature. There is no point at which the author addresses the reader directly. This is a good way of telling Kim's story, because nothing is explained; everything is experienced and enjoyed equally by the boy. He does not question the different religions or castes of India, and he does not wonder why the British rule India. These things are there to be lived through and experienced.

The structure of *Kim* is based upon a system of contrasts, and upon a series of settings.

There are very many contrasts in the book, from the contrast between youth and age, action and contemplation in the figures of Kim and the lama, to the contrast between the plains and the hills, or between the night-time scenes and the scenes in daylight. There are contrasts between the closed life of school or barracks, and the casual open life on the road. Can you list more contrasts for yourself?

The series of settings unfolds a large and varied world before the reader. The settings can be urban, as in Lucknow or Lahore, or rural, as in the fruit-gardens or in the hills. The scene can be set in the heat of the day or in the dark, cool night. It can be a wide setting on the highway of the Grand Trunk Road, or an enclosed setting in the priest's cell of the temple. A setting on the large scale is the countryside through which Kim and the lama pass on their way into the hills. This is matched by the large setting of the plains, which are Kim's first home.

The structure of *Kim* is based, too, upon journeys. Kim's different journeys are the one governing structural principle of the book. Can you bring to mind several of these journeys? You could list, for example, the events of the very first journey, which Kim and the lama made to Umballa, or their last journey together, their return from Shamlegh to the plains.

At the same time, the structure of the book is balanced, from the outside, by Kipling's having put it in three main parts. He does not say that we should do so, but we can read it as being divided into three sets of five chapters. These parts of the book are of equal length.

The first five chapters show Kim the orphan boy setting out from Lahore with the lama. At the same time he is first employed on the intelligence service. He finds his father's regiment.

The middle five chapters show Kim's training among his countrymen at school, and his training during the holidays too.

The last five chapters show Kim's testing, how he is strained by the course of events almost to breaking-point. Lurgan has tested how much he learnt with him; Mahbub has tested him over the sands to Bikanir, and in his map-work; the babu tests him as an accomplice against the Russians. All unknowing, the lama will make the greatest test of all, when Kim's love supports his master to the point of exhaustion and beyond.

To sum up, then, the reader can be recommended to think of the threefold division of Kim's youth as this: Chapters I to V, setting out; Chapters VI to X, training; Chapters XI to XV, testing and success. In the end Kim is both playing the Game and completing the Search.

The form of *Kim* is a great unfolding. Episodes are used for the function of story-telling. At every point on the line of the story we are aware of two main threads. The Game unfolds the many circumstances of human action. The Search unfolds for us the lonely quest of the spirit. Can you think of any one of Kim's actions that furthers both the Game and the Search? There is, for example, the time when he makes his journey as a grown lad of sixteen with the lama on the northbound train. He is travelling as the lama's *chela,* but he saves the life of E.23 when that secret agent enters their compartment. Recall a few other instances. The twin threads of the Game and the Search are never separated throughout the book.

The book is also constructed of different elements which recur throughout it, such as paradox, humour, pathos, perspective, and the imagery of light and landscape.

Paradox

Many situations in the story are paradoxical. We have already seen how the grand contrasts of the book work. Now look at the smaller paradoxes, where an event shows two or more opposed aspects which are both real but which are the antithesis, or opposite of one another.

For example, Kim's rescue of the Mahratta (E.23) shows a real aspect to the man himself who knows he is saved, and another aspect of the lama, who sees it as an exercise for Kim's pride, and yet another aspect to the Punjabi farmer, who is so afraid of the transformation he has seen that he leaves the train. An event can mean one thing to one person, and seem different to other people.

Kim's own character is full of paradox, because both abstract thought and concrete action appeal to him. Mahbub likes to see him dressed as a Pathan, or as a Muslim horse-boy; the babu enjoys seeing him act the part of a fakir, at Lurgan's; the lama sees him dressed as a Buddhist disciple. Beneath the different disguises stands an orphan Irish boy, the waif from Lahore, as the reader knows. These are paradoxes. And there is yet another paradox here, for Kim is not sure how he thinks of himself. Three times, in the course of the book, he asks himself 'Who is Kim?' The paradox of Kim's identity is never completely resolved.

The figure of the lama is a paradox too. The simple old man contemplating in a cell of the temple becomes the strong hillman walking his hills again.

There is a paradox in the wild figure of Mahbub Ali, the fierce Pathan. He turns out to love Kim and even to appreciate Kim's respect for the lama. We, the readers, become fond of Mahbub, and do not want to see this man who fights blood-feuds being murdered by his enemies at Umballa.

We expect the fat Bengali babu to be too afraid to be of much use in the Game. But, on the contrary, there is an element in the babu which is hardy and full of resource. He is a paradox, too.

Can you think of another event which is a paradox, for yourself? What about the last event of the book, for example? The lama has fallen into the brook and thinks his salvation is sure: the babu pulls him out and thinks he is having a fit.

Humour

There is humour in many of the paradoxical events, such as the last one. A wealth of humour fills the pages of *Kim*, whether we are laughing at the cunning which he employs to get money for a ticket, or sharing the joke against the Englishmen which only Kim, the speaker of native languages, understands fully. It is a great jest to hear the sahiba's chatter. We have a wonderful laugh when the same babu who completed the hill journey in lean hardship returns to Kim 'in highest condition of fat'. Kim does not laugh, which is a sign that he is not well yet: 'you shall laugh when you are well', says the babu, who has had a good laugh at the foreigners retreating through all the villages when 'the bottoms of their trousers were *quite* torn'. There is irony here for the spies, who thought they could handle Indians. Do other occasions come to mind, where the comic touch is clear? Mahbub and Kim love to enjoy a laugh in their conversations, for example, where Mahbub describes to Kim how one Englishman did not know his Urdu well enough to save him from using the language in a way that has been making everyone laugh at his mistake since.

Pathos

At the opposite range of feeling, we feel strong emotion for the very real struggle which is going on for the lama; it is the struggle of the spirit and the flesh. Here is the lama at Lucknow, after telling Kim that it was not out of affection that he came to watch him enter his new school. The lama, who has grown fond of his little disciple, cannot stop himself from thinking, 'maybe thou wilt forget me and our meetings'. This makes Kim cry passionately, 'If I eat thy bread, how shall I ever forget thee?', since the lama is paying for his education. The lama bids him 'Go up to the Gates of Learning. Let me see thee go . . . . Dost thou love me? Then go, or my heart cracks . . . .' After this, we feel sure that the lama will come again to see Kim, and it is a moment of great pathos, the lama staying outside the wall and hearing the Gates of Learning shut behind Kim 'with a clang'. There is pathos, too, at the time of the lama's collapse and his terrible determination to reach the plains with what little life is left to him, when he bids his native hills farewell. There is pathos, again, in the Woman of Shamlegh's affection for Kim, since, in the past, she loved a sahib who went away and never returned. Probably the most continued pathos of the book is our feeling for the lama, whose yearning to be 'set free' has to be expressed within the tradition of his ancient discipline. His strongest emotions are always contained within the words of his customary conceptual thought, and there is pathos in this.

Perspective

There are different kinds of perspective at work in the structure of the book. There are social perspectives, where each character is seen in a setting of his religion and his trade and the part of India from which he comes. A historical perspective is given when the lama talks about the journeys of Lord Buddha, which took place in the far distant past, or when the rissaldar recounts the events of the Mutiny, not so long ago.

Another kind of perspective comes from seeing each character alongside others: Kim is significant in the company of the lama; the lama has his own significance in the company of Kim.

From the crowded bazaars of Lucknow, Kim is given new direction by a perspective of the plains outside. It gives a background for his actions. The background of the story is tremendously varied and detailed. Think for yourself how many backgrounds, how many scene-settings, you can call to mind from the book. There is the Kashmir *serai,* and the sahiba's camp; there are the village communities which Kim and the lama pass through, as in the pastoral episodes of their wanderings among the little villages of the fruit-gardens. There are bazaars and railway stations: all these places are depicted as precisely as if on a map, with a selection of telling detail to complete the picture. The author knows the countryside of India like his hand. And he is sure of his railway time-tables, too.

Imagery

The background scenes involve the imagery of light which is used to such advantage throughout the book. India has a different quality of light from other countries, and Kipling is concerned to render it accurately at every time of day. Do you remember sunset on the Grand Trunk Road?

> By this time the sun was driving broad golden spokes through the lower branches of the mango-trees . . . . Swiftly the light gathered itself together, painted for an instant the faces and the cart-wheels and the bullocks' horns as red as blood. Then the night fell, changing the touch of the air, drawing a low, even haze, like a gossamer veil of blue, across the face of the country . . . .

It is like painting a picture. The following morning, we are told:

> The diamond-bright dawn woke men and crows and bullocks together . . . . The morning mist swept off in a whorl of silver, the parrots shot away to some distant river in shrieking green hosts: . . . India was awake, and Kim was in the middle of it, more awake and more excited than anyone . . . .

The poetic imagery is used to place Kim. The whole book is full of colourful lighting, from the old lady's palanquin surrounded by smoking torchlight, to Kim sitting at his master's feet, at evening, peering to see 'the cross-legged figure, outlined jet-black against the lemon-coloured drift of light'.

The imagery of landscape is at work, too, in this last scene, for we already see that where they are sitting is a little knoll with a young banyan tree, the ground being 'good clean dust'.

The abundant landscapes of *Kim* have no equal. There is every-thing of northern India in the book, from the level plains, full of fields, to the sands of the desert, rich cities, majestic hills. The careful treatment given to even a mango grove (that one where Kim is re-united with the Regiment) or a little rill of water gives reality, and we feel this also when the miraculous ending comes for the lama, which transforms the little brook into the sacred River of the Arrow.

Kipling's style is complex and makes good use of cadence and rhythm. Yet his stiff dialogue and long, involved sentences can leave us feeling that this is a blemished expression. Critics have felt his use of language to be especially strained where he gives high-flown words to the lama, or an odd manner of speaking to Mahbub Ali, for example. Yet he carries it off because he convinces us that Mahbub Ali or the lama spoke in this way. It may approximate to the way in which a Tibetan lama or a Pathan horse-dealer speaks, but the style is a success in *Kim* because it does consistently become their idiom.

Do you think it was because he was a reporter that Kipling's ideas usually flow fast? He knows what he wants to say, and therefore he says it well. This is a point to remember in your own writing.

He tries to make his conversation colloquial, the accent of living men. He succeeds particularly well with the Indian-English spoken by Kim to the sahibs he meets in the Regiment. 'Yess. That was how my father told me. My father, he has lived . . . . Of *course* he is dead – gone-out.' Even the sing-song accent can be heard in his speech.

Kipling's style is not simple, rather it is rhythmical, and exact. Exactness means he always finds the one word which expresses what he wants to say. It is crisp and clear. This is vigorous and dramatic English writing. Look at the paragraph which describes the blow struck, the lama stunned then snatched up, Kim attacking the Russian, the Frenchman fumbling at his revolver, the coolies throwing 'a shower of cutting stones' and making off up the hill 'as fast as plains-men run across the level'. The whole violent action is summed up in the final sentence of the paragraph: 'All came about as swiftly as the sudden mountain-darkness.' This is strong writing. The narrative style runs smoothly throughout. What is really good is its lively manner, which only the habit of writing constantly seems to give.

The elevated passages must also be mentioned: the wise rhetoric of the lama, for instance, or the courtly speeches of Mahbub: 'Were I Amir of Afghanistan . . . . I would fill thy mouth with gold.' Mahbub has speeches of exaggerated language along with very plain speaking: 'My son, what need of words between us?' Elevated, too, are the metaphors describing the mountains: 'All day long they lay like molten silver under the sun, and at evening put on their jewels again.' The chapters detailing the magnificence of the hills contain very grand descriptive writing.

The characters

How does Kipling reveal character in *Kim*? He sets his characters in
context, in a historical or social setting. He gives us an authentic
description of their personal appearance. Most important, he lets us
know what goes on in their minds by their words and actions. Many
characters spring out of the novel with a marvellous fertility. Here is a
detailed list of the major and minor characters, their personal
description and the role they play.

Kim, or Kimball O'Hara

When we meet him, Kim is aged about thirteen, a waif in Lahore
city, 'a poor white of the very poorest'. Orphan of a mother who
died of cholera and of a father who had been a colour-sergeant of an
Irish regiment, worked on the Railway, then died taking opium,
Kim is gifted with a great zest for life. He never forgets anything and
he learns all the time. He delights in new experiences. He is a bright
young boy, who eagerly co-operates with the training his mind receives
at school and on the Road. By the age of sixteen he is fit to play his
part in the Game, but he is also a faithful, loving disciple 'of
singular, though unwashen, beauty' to his old lama. His vigour stands
up to the testing it gets during his adventures. He becomes older and
wiser through the book. He learns his work, he suffers, he succeeds;
he learns self-respect. From being the urchin who puts his head on one
side like an Indian crow, he becomes the youth whom half India
would like to have as a son.

The lama

The Venerable Teshoo Lama, the priest of Such-Zen, is a six-foot-tall
Tibetan lama, a Red Hat Buddhist, abbot of his monastery at home,
on pilgrimage in search of the River where the Lord Buddha's arrow
fell. He hopes to be set free from the 'Wheel of Things' by finding it.
The lama also grows older during the course of the book, and the
reader understands him better as the book goes on. From seeming to be
a simple, bewildered old man adrift in a 'great and terrible World',
we see him at last as the wise, skilled abbot, calmly set on his Search and
sure of its outcome, who endures spiritual struggles and physical
hardship bravely, and who wins 'salvation for himself and his beloved'
at the end. With his wrinkled yellow face, tam o'shanter hat, the
folds of drapery that are a lama's clothes, and his tall stature, he is a
symbol of Asia itself, Asia taking Kim to its heart.

Mahbub Ali

Mahbub Ali is a horse-trader who has known Kim from his childhood days in Lahore. An old Pathan, he grows to love Kim as a son. His appearance is that of a 'big, burly Afghan, his beard dyed scarlet', who loves his hookah, visiting favourite women, and even drinking wine. He has blood-feuds of his own across the border, and is expert in horsemanship. He is also an agent for the British government. He employs Kim first to pass on information, then, when Kim succeeds in this, brings him to the notice of Colonel Creighton. Kim saves Mahbub's life, when he warns him that his enemies are lying in wait for him one night. Mahbub takes him with him on his journeys, in the guise of a favourite horse-boy. When the book ends, we know Kim will be with Mahbub 'beyond Balkh in six months', playing the Great Game.

Hurree Chunder Mookerjee

'How comes it that this man is one of us?' Kim wonders when he first meets the 'whale-like' babu. The fat Bengali appears to be a stock figure of a babu, showing off his English and hoping one day to be made a Fellow of the Royal Society in London. Yet Lurgan knows him to be 'one of the best' players of the Game. His character surprises us, and the further the book goes on the more we learn about the babu. His encounter with the foreign spies, his convincing acting, his bravery in returning to them when they are made furious by the loss of all their secret work, his cunning in making them the laughing-stock of the hill people, who will think little of foreigners in future, his endurance on long hill-marches: these are all unexpected feats from the babu. Even Kim does not recognise him at first when he plays the fakir. He can be a figure of fun, too, when he is afraid of Huneefa's sorcery, or is seen 'skipping elephantinely' for joy. At the end, he is on hand to pull the lama out of the brook.

Lurgan Sahib

Kim is sent to stay with Lurgan Sahib, the shopkeeper, in Simla. He is really 'the healer of sick pearls' who trains secret agents to be entered in government service. He respects Kim because he finds Kim is the only boy he cannot make see things (illusions) against his will. He teaches Kim the memory game, the finer art of disguise, and many other secrets that will prove useful to him on the Road. 'He was a Sahib in that he wore Sahib's clothes; the accent of his Urdu, the intonation of his English, showed that he was anything but a Sahib'. He practises magic, he knows all about the occult, he understands everything Asiatic. He is Kim's 'teacher' during the holidays.

Colonel Creighton

Colonel Creighton is the only Englishman of importance in the book, because he is the only sahib who understands Kim's potential and true value to the government. He appears to be a 'foolish Sahib' to outsiders, a colonel without a regiment, who lets himself be cheated over horses. But Kim knows he is the man to whom Kim passed his message concerning the pedigree of the white stallion, and whom he saw in secret conversation with the Commander-in-Chief. Therefore he is a man entrusted with great secrets, the player of a hidden game, 'whose eyes were so different from the dull fat eyes of other Sahibs' and who speaks fluent Urdu. Mahbub points out to the colonel that Kim could be trained just as a polo-pony is. The colonel sees at once what is meant by the metaphor. He takes over the boy from Father Victor, sees him to Lucknow, and on the way explains Kim's future career to him. When Kim is sixteen, it is Colonel Creighton who arranges for him to be taken out of school on government service, and who receives reports of his work and successes.

The sahiba

An old lady, the widow of a hill rajah, the sahiba is on pilgrimage on the Grand Trunk Road. We catch glimpses of her hidden behind curtains in the domed family bullock-cart, or borne in her palanquin around her house. She is very old, her face 'by no means lovely' but a former beauty, whose main concern is with the health of her grandson. She is 'intensely human, and lives to look upon life'. She is used to command, and has a quick tongue, and a habit of talking endlessly. The lama travelled with her as her priest for a short time. He revisits her in her home at Saharunpore on the Search. Her hospitality is as rich as her conversation. She nurses Kim back to health on his return from the hills. She admires him for his handsomeness, and loves him for the devotion he shows to the old lama.

The curator of the Lahore Museum

Modelled on Lockwood Kipling, the author's father, the curator befriends the lama and makes him a gift of his spectacles, because 'we be craftsmen together, thou and I'. Thereafter the lama thinks of him as the kind of sahib he would like Kim to be, 'wiser than many abbots'.

The rissaldar

An old soldier who had stayed loyal to the British during the Mutiny, and has been rewarded with the Order of British India and his own holding in the village. He remembers the days when he was young and strong. The lama talks to him of the Way, but Kim loves to hear his soldier's talk, though Kim himself has no wish to be a soldier. This rissaldar is a village character and a character from Indian history.

Mr Bennett

Church of England chaplain of the regiment, Bennett captures Kim outside the mess-tent, and makes a poor job of questioning him. He is a narrow-minded man, who calls Kim 'a phenomenal little liar' and looks at the Holy One 'with the triple-ringed uninterest of the creed that lumps nine-tenths of the world under the title of "heathen"'. Kipling had no fondness for regimental chaplains, or most Christians.

Father Victor

The Roman Catholic chaplain who has to be called in by Bennett to make some sense of Kim's story. He does believe Kim, at least, for he knew his father and mother, but he is at a loss what to do with the boy once he is taken over by the regiment. Yet he is keen for Kim to go to St Xavier's to receive a Catholic education (rather than let him go to the Military Orphanage) and accepts the lama's promise to pay for it.

The Kamboh

A Punjabi farmer who has come to Benares looking for a cure for his sick child. He is a big, strong man; 'the child turned on the cushion of the huge corded arms and looked at Kim through heavy eyelids'. When his child is healed by Kim he travels with the lama and his disciple to Delhi, but leaves them then since he is afraid of Kim's magic that he saw him perform on the Mahratta.

The Mahratta

E.23 has been down south on a government adventure, and, pursued for his life, tumbles into Kim's compartment, 'a mean, lean little person'. Kim and he recognise each other's amulets and way of speaking: after this contact Kim disguises E.23 as a saddhu, or holy man, and helps him escape his pursuers at the station. E.23, also trained by Lurgan, reports Kim's success.

Huneefa

The sorceress, to whose house Mahbub takes Kim when he leaves school for her spells and protection. She is 'huge and shapeless', 'decked . . . with heavy native jewellery', and she is blind with 'white sightless eyes'. She changes Kim's colour with dye, and invokes devils to give him 'the full protection of the Road'.

The Woman of Shamlegh

She rules Shamlegh-under-the-Snow, where the coolies flee to distribute their booty, since she is known not to love the sahibs. The reason for this, as she lets Kim know, is that once she loved a sahib who went away and never came back to her. She is a 'fair-coloured woman with turquoise-studded headgear' and 'bold, bright eyes'. She is very strong: she can lift a heavy basket like a toy, or go easily uphill with Kim's message to the babu. She has several husbands, and she takes a liking to Kim, whom she thinks of as 'a magician – who is like a Sahib'. She tells him the village is his, but Kim will not stay, the lama wishing to go. Kim surprises her when he leaves by thanking her with a kiss, which shows him to be an Englishman. She gives food and a litter carried by hillmen for their journey.

The Russian and the Frenchman

The two spies, who have made maps in the hills, and won hill rajahs over to the Czar their master's way of thinking. They strike the babu on the wrist, and later press drink upon him when he becomes their guide. They have bought all their 'hunting-trophies' and they have no retinue of servants, so the coolies do not trust them, knowing they are 'poor Sahibs'. Yet the Russian thinks 'It is *we* who can deal with Orientals'. He thinks the lama has 'insolent' eyes, and strikes the Holy One full in the face, bringing their own downfall on them, all because the lama will not sell his handworked chart for money. The spies make a ridiculous picture, ragged and weary, on their way to Simla. They have discredited their countrymen in the eyes of the hill-people, for the next few years, at least.

The great wealth of Kim lies in its characterisation of many of the different castes and kinds of the native peoples of India. Individuals will turn up two or three times during the story, as naturally as they would do even in a vast land like India. There is the sallow district superintendent of police, whom Kim observes first chaffing the old sahiba on the Grand Trunk Road, and recognises years later when

E.23 leaps out of the carriage to him at Delhi Station. Then there are the people Kim meets only once on his travels, each carefully described to add to the detail of the scene. Among these minor characters there are: the Hindu shopkeeper of the bazaar, who gives Kim a hot meal when he drives the bull away from her stall; the village priest who tries to steal the lama's money overnight; the drummer-boy who makes Kim's life in barracks a misery; the young letter-writer whom Kim tricks into writing to Mahbub Ali for no payment; the Hindu child-servant of Lurgan who tries to poison his master because he is jealous of Kim's arrival; the man from Ao-chung, leader of the coolies and a pet *shikarri* of sahibs, who makes off with the spies' rifle and ammunition; the cousin's widow in the sahiba's house who is skilled in massage, and helps to cure Kim.

Each portrait is executed with great detail, and there are representatives of many of the peoples of northern India. For example, on one train journey alone, we meet all the third-class passengers of Kim's compartment. There is the Hindu Jat cultivator and his wife from the rich Jullundur district, a young Dogra soldier proud of his regiment, a mean moneylender, and a generous Amritzar courtesan who gives Kim money. Kim took great pleasure in meeting new people on the Road, and Kipling's invention supplies the novel with a flourishing number of realistic characters. He describes what he has seen, in mankind in India; these are the figures we would meet today by the wayside. He is not just observing foreign peoples, but they are made real to us because they are not artificial or simplified. They speak vividly and they do not always act the way we expect.

The authenticity of the characters must be stressed since the subject matter of all novels is human relationships. In *Kim* we can observe that these relationships with other characters direct the boy's soul.

The achievement of *Kim*

What is the nature of *Kim*? It is prose fiction. It is a portrait of life in India at a particular time in history: but it also treats certain supernatural and marvellous ideas. It contains both the real and the exceptional as elements in its story. It is a masterpiece of beauty and wisdom. For example, to most European authors the lama would be a mysterious Oriental figure, not a living character as he becomes under Kipling's philosophical handling. Kim, too, is both a living character and an imaginary character; he always has some inward thought to compare with his outward actions. The spiritual and the actual elements keep pace with one another throughout the book. For example, in the ending we hear about the spiritual event which has taken place from the lama; we see it from Kim's point of view, which is *not* spiritual.

Each viewpoint heightens the significance of the other.

How was it written? We know from the life of Kipling what his early surroundings were, and how rich was the material they gave him for his books. *Kim* was the great book to come out of that experience of India. Kipling had the kind of mind that absorbed everything, and when it came to the actual writing of *Kim*, he also had the advice of his father to draw upon, in his retirement after a working life spent in India. In *Something of Myself*, Kipling talks of smoking over *Kim* with his father, and how 'the more we explored its possibilities the more opulence of detail did we discover'. He describes how '*Kim* took care of himself . . . . Between us, we knew every step, sight, and smell on his casual road, as well as all the persons he met.' Here is a clue to the composition of *Kim*, to its appeal to the senses and its wealth of characters. It is a book of memories of India, but more than that, it is a vision of India. *Kim* has been called a *given* book in *Something of Myself*; Kipling, in talking of the inspiration of his writing, said 'My Daemon was with me in . . . *Kim* . . . and good care I took to walk delicately, lest he should withdraw . . . . When your Daemon is in charge, do not try to think consciously. Drift, wait, and obey.' The book itself confirms this judgement.

Who is Kim? Three times in the course of the book Kim asks himself this question. The big question of identity is never resolved; what matters is that he should ask himself the question. Kim does not have the same kind of personal identity as the babu or the Pathan: true, he is an Irish soldier's orphan, apprenticed to become a government intelligence man. But Kim has an original nature, a talent for 'passing' as any native of India that he chooses. He can become what he is not, and go undetected where he likes. In a land where anyone's caste and creed is instantly recognisable from their physical appearance and habit of speech, Kim's ability allows him to merge with whatever society he finds himself in. Kipling, as a writer and reporter, must have longed to be able to do the same. Not many sahibs could have gone where Kim goes. When he 'passes' disguised as other people, he is the very spirit of Kipling's own night-wanderings in the old city of Lahore.

The unity of the book comes through Kim. Through his zest for life a whole world is created, as Kim travels on his way. Because Kim loves India, so does the reader. We can apply to Kim the Indian saying, 'I met a hundred men on the road to Delhi, and they were all my brothers'. Kim is popular with men of all kinds; all the people of India love him because he is young and good-looking, enterprising and vigorous. Therefore, in childhood he has the example of different kinds of men, from the lama to Mahbub Ali, who are an inspiration and a training to him. The way Kim's mind moves, he is learning all the time, and never forgets anything. He learns his work, he succeeds, he suffers, and this brings him self-respect.

Kim rejoices in being worldly. This world in itself can satisfy Kim. Do you remember the lama on the Grand Trunk Road, aloof, detached, not seeing the world he travels through, while Kim absorbs it all? Responsiveness is the keynote of Kim's nature, like the quick response of a polo-pony born to the game, one of the favourite metaphors of the book.

Nurtured by India, by her air, her water, her earth, and by her kindly, generous people, Kim responds by loving, and by acting in the service of that government which Kipling saw as preserving the peace in which the lama, the Afghan, the babu and all the small characters could live together. Kim can carry the fates of thousands 'slung round his neck'. The same night he can slip back undetected to watch as 'the big stars sailed across the dark'. Actions take place on a really large scale background. This is particularly clear as Kim's understanding of the lama deepens. From being the object of Kim's curiosity at the opening of the book, the lama is revealed as a sage at the end. Whatever Kim may choose to do with his life, the lama has made sure that salvation awaits him at its close.

What does it mean? What is the book about? It begins with Kim and the lama together, and ends with the same two figures alone. Yet we have learned everything there is to know about them. Kim represents action, human interest, the life of the senses, youth our first stage. The lama represents the achievement of wisdom in old age. Out of his spiritual battle the lama is reaching serenity. Out of the adventures of an enthusiastic youth, Kim is reaching maturity. As we grow older, we hope to grow wiser. Kim is certainly wise for his years. It is a celebration of our life.

Kim is meant to be an adventure story, for young people. Yet it is so rich, that its nearest equivalent, which is *Treasure Island* (1883) by Robert Louis Stevenson (1850–94), wonderful though it is, has none of the wealth of *Kim*.

What is Kipling's attitude to life in India? He has used Kim in a dramatic way to show us Indians in an atmosphere of complete religious and racial tolerance. He is receptive to all creeds, every kind of magic or supernatural notion. Lurgan's hypnosis or Huneefa's ritual would have been of special interest to Kipling's contemporaries, many of whom were investigating the occult at the time. The treatment given to the supernatural in the book is magical but not evil. Nothing evil persists in the story: even the action which the spies took, striking the lama and shooting at Kim and the coolies, does not bring more evil in its wake, but moves away, around on the 'Wheel of Things'.

As for the religions of India, they do not cause strife or hatred among the characters. Even Mahbub Ali, who calls down 'God's curse on all unbelievers!' when he first sees the lama, tells Kim that he is of the opinion that 'the Faiths are like the horses. Each has merit in its own country'. To which Kim makes the reply, 'But my lama said altogether a different thing'. Kim means that the lama held that there is but one Way, one Law, on the path to spiritual freedom. Mahbub Ali answers 'Oh, he is an old dreamer of dreams from Bhotiyal. My heart is a little angry, Friend of all the World, that thou shouldst see such worth in a man so little known.' Clearly, the lama is not enough of a man of action for tough old Mahbub's liking. Kim quickly replies, 'It is true, Hajji; but that worth do I see, and to him my heart is drawn'. He shows his respect for Mahbub by using the honoured name of Hajji, the title given only to one who has already been on pilgrimage to Mecca. But Kim still says his heart is with the lama. When Mahbub smiles at the thought of the lama like a beggar in the presence of the young sahibs at the school, where he comes to visit Kim, Kim scornfully says the young sahibs are 'brothers-in-law to the *bhungi* [sweeper]'. To Kim's way of thinking, they are of no worth compared to the lama. Kim sees through outward appearances to the man's heart.

There is, then, one reason for Kim's choosing his own way of life: he loves, and wants to be with, Indians. His friendships with many different Indian people are the material of the book. Most English writers of Kipling's time, because of social taboos, would have shied away from such subject matter. But in *Kim* these friendships are made possible by the boy's character. By the end of the book the characters, as well as the country, appear in a three-dimensional way to us: we really know them. The outlandish figure of the lama in his foreign clothes and huge hat, his yellow colour and wrinkled eyes, becomes well-known and well-loved. We know what he must look like after his journeys and meditations. By the last chapter we can imagine what his face is like after the ultimate experience of compassion. We see his mildness, yet understand his interior toughness, like that of his Master the Lord Buddha, who, as a prince, rode away from Kapilivastu, leaving wife and child behind him. It is Kim and the lama together who give this book its first place in English literature about India; they give it the resounding truth of one of the *Jâtakas*, those earliest of Indian tales about the life of the Buddha. The *Jâtaka* is the oriental ancestor of *Kim*. Like India itself, *Kim* is both ancient and vitally new.

Is *Kim* a great book? Yes, for we have a real experience in it. The reality is that of the person who is living the long adventure told in the book. Kim's insight is ours; like him, we are always understanding more of ourselves and of other people. It is a celebration of a boy's mind, a mind which finds all events intelligible. We readers can find ourselves and our own world in it. It is a work of art, since it illuminates life.for us here and now.

Part 4

Hints for study

THESE HINTS FOR STUDY are intended to help you to pass an examination. Remember that it is up to you to make it clear to the examiner that you have a good understanding of the text. To this end, it is necessary to have read the original text itself at least twice, then to think about it for yourself and to join in conversation about it, not only in your classes but at other times, too. To help you to express yourself clearly, the following procedures will be helpful.

(i) Select points for detailed study

Choose a topic such as theme, or character, and study its development throughout the book. Make a selection of happenings, or ways of looking at events, which throw light on your chosen topics. List all the relevant information systematically, in order to be able to revise your work quickly just before the examination. For example, in describing the theme of *Kim,* it would help you to list its thematic essentials in this way:

Early boyhood, becoming the lama's friend and disciple at the same time as setting out on a mission for an older friend, Mahbub Ali;

Kim's wanderings, and his finding of the Red Bull regiment;

Kim, selected to play the Great Game as a career, receives his education at the lama's expense;

Youth, taking the Road again with the lama, but still joining in secret service work;

The climax of the book, the adventure with the Russian spies, the return to the plains, the finding of the lama's River.

To take another example, in talking about character, go over the detailed list of major and minor characters to refresh your memory. Make sure you can recall the human relationships in which your particular character was involved, and try to see what the driving force is which makes the character act as he does. Then you can describe him in terms of his personal appearance, his speech and his actions. Show how authentic, how 'well-rounded' the character is. Is he a person you feel you have known, through reading the book?

Select your own points and fill in information about them in the manner just indicated. The following is a useful list: theme, character, relationships, conflict of emotions, setting, climax, rhetoric, imagery, humour, journeys.

(ii) Select suitable quotations to illustrate characters or highlights of the book

Choose and commit to memory some quotations which illustrate the major concerns of the book. A quotation may be useful because of the liveliness or immediacy of its language, or because of the light it casts on an event or a character, or because of the beauty or wisdom of its expression. It may be a single word, like 'loot', from the very first paragraph of *Kim*. This is a useful word to pick out because it is an Indian word meaning 'plunder', long familiar in Anglo-Indian speech. It is an apt word because it calls to mind India's history, her conquerors, and the riches we expect to find in the east. Or you may choose to remember a phrase, such as 'This great and beautiful land', which is Kim's reply to Mahbub's question in Chapter VIII, 'And who are thy people, Friend of all the World?'. This answer shows the breadth of Kim's youthful vision of the world, *and* how he thinks of the country and its people as one and the same thing.

Equally revealing would be single sentences like the lama's 'Alas! It is a great and terrible world' in Chapter II, or Mahbub's 'God's curse on all unbelievers!' in Chapter I. These say much about their speakers.

Or you might select an extract from a longer passage, as in this description of a halt on the Grand Trunk Road at dawn, which indicates how life appears through Kim's eyes. 'Kim sat up and yawned, shook himself, and thrilled with delight. This was seeing the world in real truth; this was life as he would have it – bustling and shouting, the buckling of belts, and beating of bullocks and creaking of wheels, lighting of fires and cooking of food, and new sights at every turn of the approving eye'. Here the passage is a useful one because it could be used to illustrate Kipling's language, the repetitive rhythms of his prose which is like verse in places.

Make up a page full of suitable quotations chosen by yourself, all specific examples drawn from the book in order to make an important point clear. Be sure you have a clear idea of where and when each quotation appears, and know how to use it. It would be useful, for example, to make a short list of the Indian words that Kim uses often, such as 'Oh, *shabash*', meaning 'well done!', and *'chela'*, meaning disciple. They indicate a use of language which shows how completely Kim embraces the Indian way of life.

(iii) Answer questions effectively

When revising, recall the main points in your notes. Do not think of revision as mere memorising. Reconstruct what you have learned in your mind, and new ideas will suggest themselves to you. (A good last-minute revision is to skim through a piece of the text or some notes, and then add up, to yourself, how much you have gathered from it.)

You ought to read *Kim* itself at least twice; the first time, in rapid reading; the second time, in study reading. Read it intensively. This means becoming very familiar with the text. Remember the main ideas, and how they connect with each other. Find significant details, and relate these to the overall structure. How do they belong to it? Read slowly, at times. Pause to think about what you are reading. Go back and reread sections of the text. Think of the sound of the prose; if you don't like the look of a passage, or can't follow it, read it aloud and you will understand it more easily.

Revise by topic, and write brief answers to questions you imagine you might be asked. Your writing will improve with this practice, and it will point to those questions where you still have to go in search of information which you lack. You will lose out, though, if you try to 'spot' definite questions; this is too risky. Use the list of likely questions in these notes to refer to sections in the earlier part of the notes which will help you to answer them. Look at past papers, too, if they are available, to find the kind of question you are likely to see on the day. This will prepare you for the examination, and make you see it as your chance to show what you have learned. It is a test of memory, of quick thinking, and of good writing at speed.

At examination time it helps to know what is expected of your answer. In any essay in answer to an examination question you are being asked for a critical account of some part of *Kim* which you have studied closely. You will probably be able to express your personal judgement at some point in your answer, at the same time as showing that you are aware of the general critical opinions on the topic under discussion.

The main requirements in your written answer will be: show your knowledge; write on the set topic; make what you write quite clear to any reader; see that your answer coheres or 'hangs together'; do some original thinking, if you can; use the best written language to prove that you are literate.

The examiner will want to know that you understand what the question is asking of you, and that you have a definite reply for him which shows you know what the set book is about.

Effective answering consists of organising and relating. Do not forget that writing itself is made much easier when the subject matter has been organised.

Many students spend all their time in an examination scribbling wildly in an effort to put down as much as possible. If you spend your time trying to dash down all you know about *Kim*, you will miss the meaning of the question-and-answer system. Keep calm and find the right questions to answer, first of all. Read and reread the *instructions to the candidate*, such as, 'Answer any 4 questions', and so on. Then you will do the right thing. Try not to choose a question whose subject does not suit you. You know the breadth of your own knowledge best. Do not choose a subject that is too difficult. Think ahead to what an answer will involve. Try to find a question which is directing your thinking already. Do you know what you want to say? Read and re-read the question to make sure you have understood what is wanted. Do not misread your questions; it is easily done.

When the examination is actually in progress, and you have found your questions, prepare to answer them exactly. Make a fair division of time between the questions. Keep track of the time, keep to what you decided was best and do not give too much of your time to any one question.

Regard each question as something to be thought about. Think about the relevance of the question you have just read to the book you know so well; ask yourself what points in the book are vital to an answer here. Is the question trying to find out what you know of one special aspect of characterisation, say? Treat a question as a sign, indicating which part of the book, or behaviour of a character, you should go back to. Call to mind everything you can about an incident or a character *before* you begin to write. Summon up all the information which will help you to answer in a relevant way.

Look for cues to the meaning of the question such as 'examine in detail', or 'summarise'. See if you have spotted any problems in answering this question. It will be easier if you think them through before writing.

Decide in advance what shape your answer will take. Make brief notes on the following principles:

In an answer plan, perhaps in pencil on a rough page, sketch out in note form how your discussion will proceed.

Follow the structure of the question closely. Identify what is being asked.

Be selective: your essay must contain the points that answer the question.

Jot down in short statements the line of your answer. A few headings will do. These should be well spaced. You may want to add a diagram to help, for example:

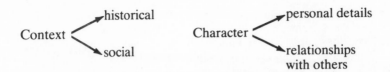

This keeps your plan in the swiftest and most economical form. You may fill it in with a full line or a quotation.

Do not hesitate too long before your write out the full and proper answer. You must not take up too much of your time with the plan. Allow yourself only five minutes for organisation of the first rough stage. It is only a skeleton that will be filled out when you write your answer.

Now start writing. Make the overall point of your answer clear and simple. Check that you have really understood what is wanted, and give the examiner the answer that is called for. Decide whether it will be of approximately the right length.

Give shape to your ideas. Make them relevant. Make them 'hang together'. Do not lose hold of the sense of what you are writing. When you have finished writing, you should have a few minutes left to check it through carefully. Let no uncorrected errors pass. You know, yourself, the kinds of mistakes you are likely to have made.

Specimen questions and model answers

The following questions are of the type that might be set in an examination. You must not regard them as covering all the questions which could be asked. There is an inexhaustible number of questions to which a book like *Kim* gives rise. These are intended to let you test your knowledge of *Kim* in general and in detail.

(1) What are the basic elements Kipling used in constructing *Kim*?
(2) Give at least one reason why *Kim* is an outstanding book.
(3) Is *Kim* written in the form that other novels took which were being written at the same time?
(4) How would you persuade a friend that *Kim* was worth reading?
(5) Explain briefly the theme of *Kim* and show how the book deals with its theme.
(6) What is there in Rudyard Kipling's own life story which suggests that he had a special interest in writing about a childhood as unusual as Kim's?
(7) In what ways do Kipling's experiences (*a*) as a child, OR (*b*) as a journalist, influence his writing?
(8) What qualities in *Kim* do you think make it the best novel about India written by an Englishman?

(9) What general meaning has Kipling attached to the Search and to the Great Game?

(10) How does Kipling set scenes? How does he use words to describe places and the moods they arouse in human beings?

(11) Why should Kipling use the imagery of light so much?

(12) Is a reader new to Kipling quick to overcome the difficulties of his style?

(13) Where does Kim, by his own doing, give us the first indications of his character?

(14) Do you see a special significance in Kim's self-questioning, and why does it appear and reappear in the book?

(15) How does Kim keep making friends so rapidly with all sorts of people? Give examples.

(16) In what ways do you feel the increasing maturity of Kim is shown?

(17) What is the lama's role in the book?

(18) What is Kim's relationship to Mahbub Ali?

(19) Contrast the personalities of the lama and Mahbub Ali, and indicate if any relationship exists between the two.

(20) What is the significance of Hurree Babu's experience when he becomes guide to the Russian and the Frenchman?

(21) What special significance does the final conversation between Kim and the lama hold for you?

(22) In some detail illustrate from earlier and later chapters the character and spiritual anguish of the lama.

(23) Relate the circumstances leading up to the orphan of the streets becoming 'a boy of St Xavier's'.

Here are four specimen answers, two of which are general answers, and two answers to content and context-type questions.

Which of the characters in *Kim* has appealed to you most strongly? (Give quotations or close references where possible)

Of all the characters in *Kim*, it is Mahbub Ali who appeals to me most strongly. He is a wild Afghan horse-dealer, an informant for the British, who has news of what goes on beyond the Khyber Pass in the rough north country. Kipling himself knew a real Mahbub Ali, in his Indian days, and I feel as if I have known him too, through reading the book. The British in India always seem to have admired the Pathan tribesmen for their proud, warlike nature, and it may be that Kipling put such a character into his book because of this appeal.

Mahbub Ali is an older man but does not show his age. In physical appearance he is big and burly, deep-chested, with 'his beard dyed scarlet with lime (for he was elderly and did not wish his grey hairs to show)'. He wears Pathan dress with a deep embroidered belt, and smokes a silver hookah. His interests seem to be horses and women, but because of his secret work, his voice is 'harsh with suspicion' and he is swift to think and to act. That is why he is still alive, although he is likely to die by violence at any time. He has his family blood-feuds, and he has in his possession when we meet him first, in the Kashmir Serai, a report beside which 'Dynamite was milky and innocuous'.

Apart from the hardships of his way of life, leading his caravan through the snows or burning sands, he leads a spy's dangerous life, and needs to be 'as prompt as he was unscrupulous', ready to take all sorts of chances, as he does when he trusts Kim with the message of the white stallion's pedigree.

He speaks his 'own picturesque language' and calls himself 'a horse-coper'. He is much amused by Kim's wit and can laugh aloud at it: 'The dealer laughed till he nearly fell from his horse'. He keeps a different tone of voice for Europeans, not the one he uses to Kim. He knows the British so well he can make use of them for his own ends, as when he lays a complaint about thieves at the station, and so rids himself of the men who wait to murder him. He is concerned for his own honour and reputation, but helps Kim by introducing him to Colonel Creighton on Umballa racecourse, saying 'He was born in the land' and so making Kim's fortune.

Kim loves him, and tells him so in Umballa. Mahbub recognises their bond of love, and says 'Our lives lie in each other's hand'. They will take the road together many times. On the road Mahbub calls Kim 'My son' and gives him a dress of honour, calling him a Pathan.

Mahbub understands that 'Hearts are like horses. They come and they go against bit or spur'. He recognises that Kim, although young, is ready for real life, and urges Colonel Creighton in Chapter X, 'Let him out – let him go' and reminds the Colonel Sahib that 'When I was fifteen, I had shot my man and begot my man, Sahib'. The Colonel thinks of Mahbub as a 'crafty old sinner' but takes his advice.

Mahbub does feel indignant that Kim should be so devoted to the old lama, but he checks this anger, saying to himself in his own tongue, Pushtu, at the close of the book, 'But the madman is fond of the boy; and I must be very reasonably mad too'. He thinks better of the lama when he hears that he once harmed a man with his pencase. None of the lama's beliefs affect Mahbub.

Mahbub is the first man Kim comes to when he takes to the Road, and his journeys over India with his string of horses broaden the scope of our knowledge. Every reader enjoys Kim's meetings with Mahbub, whether they take place at the Kashmir Serai, on Umballa racecourse, in the city or on the road. I like him for his fierce exterior and tender heart, and the possibility of hasty action that he always brings with him, galloping on his 'grey Kabuli stallion'.

By referring to three incidents show the meaning of the Great Game
for Kim

Three incidents which show the meaning of the Great Game are: Kim's
delivery of the message concerning the pedigree of the white stallion;
Kim's rescue of secret agent E.23; Kim's capture of the documents
from the foreign spies.

When Kim first looks for work to get money for himself and the lama,
he does not suspect that Mahbub Ali is 'registered in one of the locked
books of the Indian Survey Department as C.25 . . . .' Yet he
understands that he will be doing a service to Mahbub Ali, and that the
message on tissue-paper wrapped in oilskin, which he finds in the bread
Mahbub gives him, is to be a secret one. He certainly does not believe
that it really has anything to do with a white stallion. Then Kim draws
new conclusions from seeing a man searching through Mahbub's boxes
and bags. Kim leaves immediately with 'the thing that I carry to
Umballa'. He knows more of its value now, since 'Those who search
bags with knives may presently search bellies with knives'.

Kim finds the house in Umballa, and speaks to the Englishman from
the darkness of the garden. As soon as Mahbub Ali's name is
mentioned, he can see that the man knows what is meant. Kim
delivers the paper, but stays behind, hidden in the garden-grass to
watch its result. He hears his sahib and the Commander-in-Chief
discuss the matter and decide that it is to be war. This is big news to
Kim, the news of armies and guns. It is Kim's first clue as to the
greatness of the Game.

By the time he rescues E.23, years have passed and Kim has been
entered into the Game by his training. As yet, he has not taken part in
it since the night when he saved Mahbub's life. When the Mahratta
enters Kim's compartment they recognise one another immediately
by their amulets and set way of speaking. Kim is thrilled to think that
this is the Great Game 'with a vengeance'. The Mahratta talks of 'us',
meaning all the spies of the Game. One has been murdered in the
south, and the Mahratta himself is a marked man with no escape. Kim
asks if the government will protect him, but the Mahratta replies 'We
of the Game are beyond protection'. Kim says he must be safe in the
train, but the reply is 'Live a year at the Great Game and tell me that
again!' Kim uses his wits and disguises E.23 as a saddhu. He escapes
his pursuers at Delhi station, all because of Kim, who is 'But two
days entered to the Game, brother'. Kim is elated by his first success.

By the time Kim is backing up the resourceful Hurree Babu, who has
attached himself as a guide to the Russian and French spies, he is really
watching the babu for signs of how they can outwit the foreigners.

Kim feels he is still a beginner at the Game, although his rescue of the Mahratta has been praised. The incident between the foreigners and the lama, as a result of which the coolies, Kim and the lama make off with all the baggage, in fact happens without anyone planning it. Kim takes swift advantage of the situation by telling the simple coolies that he can draw out the magic of the red *kilta*, 'full of very wonderful things, not to be handled by fools'. He extracts the maps and documents from it, and throws the unnecessary things over Shamlegh-midden. He is proud to think of the collapse of the foreigners' own Great Game. But on the return to the plains the responsibility of the papers weighs heavily on Kim. He has matured, for he feels the secrets as a burden, and longs to pass them on to the government. He is glad when he is rid of them and Hurree has taken them away. At last he fully understands the Great Game; he knows about treason, secret information, danger and the credit of a good report for his work.

Here are summarised answers to two context questions:

'From time to time, God causes men to be born – and thou art one of them – who have a lust to go abroad at the risk of their lives and discover news – today it may be of far-off things, tomorrow of some hidden mountain, and the next day of some near-by men who have done a foolishness against the State. These souls are very few; and of these few, not more than ten are of the best. Among these ten I count the babu, and that is curious. How great, therefore, and desirable must be a business that brazens the heart of a Bengali!'

(a) Briefly describe the circumstances giving rise to this speech
(b) Comment on the words 'who have a lust to go abroad at the risk of their lives and discover news'
(c) Give the meaning of the last sentence of the extract
(d) Say who said this, and on what occasion

(*a*) Kim is staying with Lurgan Sahib, to be trained in the Great Game. He is learning how to be a secret agent and yet stay alive.

(*b*) These words describe the temperament of the kind of man who can become an intelligence agent. He must have a keen desire to take to the road, even though he is always in danger of death from his enemies, for the sake of finding information.

(*c*) This sentence impresses on us the greatness of the Game, since it makes even a Bengali like the babu, who is renowned for his timidity, act bravely.

(*d*) Lurgan says this, in reply to Kim's wondering how the babu can disguise himself or talk other languages, and what his pay can be, if anyone who might betray him could earn a thousand rupees or more. Kim has only just met the babu.

'I acquire merit in that I help thee, my *chela*, to wisdom. The priest of that body of men who serve the Red Bull wrote me that all should be as I desired for thee. I sent the money to suffice for one year, and then I came, as thou seest me, to watch for thee going up into the Gates of Learning. A day and a half have I waited – not because I was led by any affection towards thee – that is no part of the Way – but, as they said at the Tirthankars' Temple, because, money having been paid for learning, it was right that I should oversee the end of the matter. They resolved my doubts most clearly. I had a fear that, perhaps, I came because I wished to see thee – misguided by the Red Mist of affection. It is not so . . . .'

(*a*) Who is speaking, and to whom?

(*b*) Explain the meaning of 'the Red Mist of affection'

(*c*) Point out the contrasting emotions felt by the speaker. Give one example from another part of the book where a passage is expressing contradictions.

(*a*) The lama is speaking to his young disciple, Kim.

(*b*) By this phrase the lama means all those ties of human emotion which blind us in our search for spiritual truth.

(*c*) The lama wants to see Kim entering his school for the first time, and he also simply wants to see the boy again. But his scruples about being fond of Kim, which is 'no part of the Way', have made him take counsel from the priests in the temple about what he ought to do. They seem to have been understanding, for they have advised him to 'oversee' Kim entering the school. The dignified logic of the lama's speech contrasts with the sentence 'I had a fear that, perhaps, I came because I wished to see thee . . .' where the rhythms of the sentence indicate the troubles of his loving spirit which longs to see Kim again.

Another passage in the book which deals in contradictions is Mahbub Ali's conversation with Colonel Creighton on the racecourse, when Mahbub is explaining who Kim is. He can say something about Kim which convinces the boy that he is destined to live a life in barracks, but the same detail can convey to Colonel Creighton that Kim is unique and must not be wasted. Kim thinks Mahbub mocks him, saying that he will forget all he knows, but it is really a sign to the colonel to become the boy's patron before it is too late. This passage decides Kim's fate, though he does not realise it at the time.

Part 5

Suggestions for further reading

The text

Kim was first published by Macmillan, London, 1901. These notes use the text published by Pan Books, London, in association with Macmillan, London, 1976. The Pan Classic edition has an introduction and additional notes by Mark Kincead-Weekes, and a useful glossary of Indian words and place-names.

Other works by Kipling

1881 *Schoolboy Lyrics.*
1886 *Departmental Ditties*
1888 *Plain Tales from the Hills*
1890 *Soldiers Three*
1890 *Wee Willie Winkie*
1889 *From Sea to Sea*
1890 *The Light that Failed*
1891 *Life's Handicap*
1892 *The Naulakha*
1892 *Barrack-Room Ballads*
1893 *Many Inventions*
1894 *The Jungle Book*
1895 *The Second Jungle Book*
1896 *The Seven Seas*
1897 *Captains Courageous*
1898 *The Day's Work*
1899 *Stalky & Co.*
1901 *Kim*

1902 *Just So Stories*
1903 *The Five Nations*
1904 *Traffics and Discoveries*
1906 *Puck of Pook's Hill*
1909 *Actions and Reactions*
1910 *Rewards and Fairies*
1913 *Letters of Travel*
1917 *A Diversity of Creatures*
1919 *The Years Between*
1923 *Land and Sea Tales*
1923 *The Irish Guards in the Great War*
1926 *Debits and Credits*
1927 *Brazilian Sketches*
1930 *Thy Servant a Dog*
1932 *Limits and Renewals*
1937 *Something of Myself* (posthumously published)

Biography

CARRINGTON, CHARLES: *Rudyard Kipling, his Life and Work,* Macmillan, London, 1978.
BIRKENHEAD, LORD: *Rudyard Kipling,* Weidenfeld and Nicolson, London, 1978.

Criticism

TOMPKINS, J.M.S.: *The Art of Rudyard Kipling,* Methuen, London, 1959.

DOBREE, BONAMY: *Rudyard Kipling, Realist and Fabulist,* Oxford University Press, London, 1967.

RUTHERFORD, ANDREW (ED.): *Kipling's Mind and Art,* Oliver & Boyd, Edinburgh and London, 1964.

WILSON, ANGUS: *The Strange Ride of Rudyard Kipling,* Secker & Warburg, London, 1977.

The author of these notes

VALERIE GILLIES was born in Canada and educated at the University of Edinburgh and at the University of Mysore, South India, where she held a Commonwealth Scholarship. A selection of her poetry was published in *Poetry Introduction 3,* Faber and Faber, London, 1975, and her first solo collection of poems appeared under the title *Each Bright Eye,* published by Canongate, Edinburgh, 1977.

She works as a freelance scriptwriter for the BBC, writing and introducing poetry programmes and dramatising scripts for schools' radio. She is one of the editors of the 1978 volume of Scottish Short Stories published by Collins. For 1978 and 1979 she was the Writer in residence at one of Lothian Region's schools in Edinburgh.

The first 100 titles

CHINUA ACHEBE

Arrow of God
Things Fall Apart

JANE AUSTEN

Northanger Abbey
Pride and Prejudice
Sense and Sensibility

ROBERT BOLT

A Man For All Seasons

CHARLOTTE BRONTË

Jane Eyre

EMILY BRONTË

Wuthering Heights

ALBERT CAMUS

L'Etranger (The Outsider)

GEOFFREY CHAUCER

Prologue to the Canterbury Tales
The Franklin's Tale
The Knight's Tale
The Nun's Priest's Tale
The Pardoner's Tale

SIR ARTHUR CONAN DOYLE

The Hound of the Baskervilles

JOSEPH CONRAD

Nostromo

DANIEL DEFOE

Robinson Crusoe

CHARLES DICKENS

David Copperfield
Great Expectations

GEORGE ELIOT

Adam Bede
Silas Marner
The Mill on the Floss

T.S. ELIOT

The Waste Land

WILLIAM FAULKNER

As I Lay Dying

F. SCOTT FITZGERALD

The Great Gatsby

E.M. FORSTER

A Passage to India

ATHOL FUGARD

Selected Plays

MRS GASKELL	*North and South*
WILLIAM GOLDING	*Lord of the Flies*
OLIVER GOLDSMITH	*The Vicar of Wakefield*
THOMAS HARDY	*Jude the Obscure* *Tess of the D'Urbervilles* *The Mayor of Casterbridge* *The Return of the Native* *The Trumpet Major*
L.P. HARTLEY	*The Go-Between*
ERNEST HEMINGWAY	*For Whom the Bell Tolls* *The Old Man and the Sea*
ANTHONY HOPE	*The Prisoner of Zenda*
RICHARD HUGHES	*A High Wind in Jamaica*
THOMAS HUGHES	*Tom Brown's Schooldays*
HENRIK IBSEN	*A Doll's House*
HENRY JAMES	*The Turn of the Screw*
BEN JONSON	*The Alchemist* *Volpone*
D.H. LAWRENCE	*Sons and Lovers* *The Rainbow*
HARPER LEE	*To Kill a Mocking-Bird*
SOMERSET MAUGHAM	*Selected Short Stories*
HERMAN MELVILLE	*Billy Budd* *Moby Dick*
ARTHUR MILLER	*Death of a Salesman* *The Crucible*
JOHN MILTON	*Paradise Lost I & II*
SEAN O'CASEY	*Juno and the Paycock*
GEORGE ORWELL	*Animal Farm* *Nineteen Eighty-four*
JOHN OSBORNE	*Look Back in Anger*
HAROLD PINTER	*The Birthday Party*
J.D. SALINGER	*The Catcher in the Rye*

SIR WALTER SCOTT	*Ivanhoe*
	Quentin Durward
WILLIAM SHAKESPEARE	*A Midsummer Night's Dream*
	Antony and Cleopatra
	Coriolanus
	Cymbeline
	Hamlet
	Henry IV Part I
	Henry V
	Julius Caesar
	King Lear
	Macbeth
	Measure for Measure
	Othello
	Richard II
	Romeo and Juliet
	The Merchant of Venice
	The Tempest
	The Winter's Tale
	Troilus and Cressida
	Twelfth Night
GEORGE BERNARD SHAW	*Androcles and the Lion*
	Arms and the Man
	Caesar and Cleopatra
	Pygmalion
RICHARD BRINSLEY SHERIDAN	*The School for Scandal*
JOHN STEINBECK	*Of Mice and Men*
	The Grapes of Wrath
	The Pearl
ROBERT LOUIS STEVENSON	*Kidnapped*
	Treasure Island
JONATHAN SWIFT	*Gulliver's Travels*
W.M. THACKERAY	*Vanity Fair*
MARK TWAIN	*Huckleberry Finn*
	Tom Sawyer
VOLTAIRE	*Candide*
H.G. WELLS	*The History of Mr Polly*
	The Invisible Man
	The War of the Worlds
OSCAR WILDE	*The Importance of Being Earnest*